THE PENGUIN DICTIONARY
OF MICROPROCESSORS

Anthony Chandor was educated at Epsom College and New College, Oxford. A Fellow of the British Computer Society, he serves on various committees of the Society including the Examinations Board for professional qualifications. In over twenty years of systems and computer management experience he has twice been appointed by the United Nations as data processing adviser. He is a member of the computing panels of the Science Research Council and the Council for National Academic Awards and is currently Managing Director of Aregon International Limited, the information systems company. He is the author of *A Short Introduction to Computers*, *Computers as a Career*, *Practical Systems Analysis* (with Graham and Williamson), *Choosing and Keeping Computer Staff* and *The Penguin Dictionary of Computers*.

THE PENGUIN
DICTIONARY OF
Microprocessors

ANTHONY CHANDOR

PENGUIN BOOKS

Penguin Books Ltd, Harmondsworth, Middlesex, England
Penguin Books, 625 Madison Avenue, New York, New York 10022, U.S.A.
Penguin Books Australia Ltd, Ringwood, Victoria, Australia
Penguin Books Canada Ltd, 2801 John Street, Markham, Ontario, Canada L3R 1B4
Penguin Books (N.Z.) Ltd, 182–190 Wairau Road, Auckland 10, New Zealand

—

First published 1981
Reprinted 1981

—

—

Filmset, printed and bound in Great Britain by
Hazell Watson & Viney Ltd, Aylesbury, Bucks
Set in VIP Times Roman

PREFACE

Microprocessors have brought computers firmly – although often unobtrusively – into all our lives, and the language of the microprocessor user is becoming increasingly a part of everyday language – 'chips with everything' is a well-understood statement of fact in two ways. The computer industry generated many exciting new words and phrases for itself, and many of these have been adapted and given new meanings in a microprocessor context. But a number of the new concepts have needed completely new words and PROM-zapping, hex pad, hot chassis and mother board take their place beside the well-established bug, bootstrap and deadly embrace. Edge card means something quite different to a microprocessor user from a punched card with notches cut at the edge (the data processing computer version) while 'inputting input by means of an input' has a familiar (if somewhat pedestrian) ring to both. Meanwhile the dreaded intermittent error ('A sporadic error which tends to occur before and after any attempt to establish its presence and cause') continues to haunt engineers and users of almost any mechanical, hydraulic or electronic device.

This book does not seek to provide a preferred definition: its objective is to be a helpful comparison in any discussion of microprocessors, and therefore all words and meanings qualify for inclusion, whether they seem elegant or not. The only rules are that strict alphabetical order is followed (ignoring commas, hyphens, etc) and words are listed in natural English order: slow death appears under S, not D. (Reversed phrases are listed only when the natural order might be hard to find.) New words and new meanings emerge joyously in the microprocessor industry to give meaning to new concepts, and I shall welcome notification from readers of new uses for old words and new words for new ideas.

Haslemere, 1980   ANTHONY CHANDOR

ACKNOWLEDGEMENT

So many people and organizations have been helpful in suggesting and explaining words that it would be wrong to acknowledge the help of only a few, but it would also be wrong not to pay an especial tribute to the group known in the computing industry as Le Micro, and, with many thanks to its members, I am glad to pay such a tribute. I know, too, that the members of Le Micro will understand my wish to give particular thanks to the Director of Publications at Urwick Nexos Ltd.

NOTE

A

abend To halt a computer run before it has reached a successful conclusion – to make an *ab*ortive *end*.

aberration An error condition, usually in the cathode ray tube of a *terminal*.

abnormal termination The ending of a computer *run*, *routine* or *program* because of a malfunction or error condition.

abort To abandon an activity in recognition of an error condition.

absolute address The physical location of storage assigned for data. The location is defined in *machine code*.
Also known as actual address, direct address, first-level address, machine address, one-level address, specific address.

absolute addressing The addressing of a physical location in storage by its *absolute address*.

absolute code *Program instructions* which have been written using *absolute addresses*. Instructions in absolute code are intelligible to a processor without the need for any intermediate processing.
Also known as actual code, basic code, direct code, one-level code and specific code.

absolute loader A *program* with the function of *loading* another program at a specified *address*.

A-bus The primary internal *bus* of a *microprocessor*.

acceleration time The time elapsing between the interpretation of a *read* or *write instruction* to a *peripheral unit* and the moment when transfer of data begins.
Also known as start time.

acceptance test A series of actions carried out to prove that a system (*hardware* and *software*) meets agreed criteria, e.g. that the processing of specified input produces expected results. ⟡ *commission*.

access To obtain data from a *storage device* or from a *peripheral unit*.

access arm The positioning device of the reading or writing mechanism of a *storage* unit.

access time The time taken from the moment of executing an *instruction* to call for data to the moment when the data has been stored in the appropriate *location*. The data may be held in a *storage device* or obtained from a *peripheral unit*, and different devices require different access times. For example, *magnetic tape* has a longer access time than *magnetic disk*.

accordion A *printed circuit* connector contact. The spring has an accordion-like Z shape to allow great deflection without the risk of over-stressing.

accumulator A *storage location* in which *operations* are performed on numbers and where the results are stored. An accumulator can act as an *arithmetic and logic unit*, and is sometimes used to control or *modify* a quantity held in another storage location. Usually it will store one value, receive another value and then hold the result of operations carried out on the original number and the second number.
Also known as accumulator register.

accumulator register Synonymous with *accumulator*.

accuracy A measure of the size of an error or the quality of freedom from error. High accuracy implies a low degree of error, and may be contrasted with *precision*. For example, a calculation to five places of decimals may be more precise than a calculation to four places of decimals, but if the five-place calculation contains an error, it will be less accurate than a four-place calculation which is error-free.

acoustic coupler A device capable of transmitting and receiving *audio* tones which can be sent on telephone lines, allowing a *modem* to be linked to a telephone handset.

acoustic delay line A *delay line* based on the time of propagation of sound waves, so that a pattern of sound pulses is launched at one end of an acoustic medium such as quartz and picked up at the other end. This means that a *binary digit* can be represented by the presence or absence of a short high-frequency *packet*.
Also known as sonic delay line.

acoustic memory Synonymous with *acoustic store*.

acoustic store A *regenerative memory* using an *acoustic delay line*.
Also known as acoustic memory.

active element A circuit which receives energy from two or more sources. One of these sources of energy controls the energy flow of the other source(s).

activity 1. The act of using a *file* of information, either by altering it or referring to it. The activity level of a file is therefore an indication of the frequency of use. 2. The representation in *PERT* and *critical path* analysis of a task or constraint. Time and/or resources are consumed and the activity is necessary in order to move from one *event*[2] to another.

actual address Synonymous with *absolute address*.

actual code Synonymous with *absolute code*.

actual instruction An *instruction* resulting from *modification* of a *basic instruction*.
Also known as effective instruction.

ADA A *high-level language* for *real time* processing problems; named after Lady Lovelace, Babbage's friend and recorder.

addend One of the *operands* used in carrying out the function of *addition*. The addend is a number which is added to another number called the *augend*, producing a result called the *sum*.

adder A device capable of performing the function of *addition* using digital signals. It receives three inputs (representing *addend*, *augend* and a *carry* digit) and will provide two outputs (representing the *sum* and a carry digit).
Also known as digital adder; it is sometimes more precisely known as a full adder, to distinguish it from *half-adder*. The term adder usually implies *three-input adder* and full adder.

adder-subtracter A device which acts as either an *adder* or a *subtracter*.

addition An arithmetic operation which produces the sum of two *operands* – the *addend* and *augend*.

additional character Synonymous with *special character*.

addition record A new *record* added to a *file* during *updating*, without causing the amendment or deletion of an existing record.

addition without carry Synonymous with *Exclusive-Or operation*.
⟡ *Boolean algebra, logic.*

address 1. An identification by a name, label or tag of a *register*, *storage location* or other source or destination of data. 2. Used as a verb, to indicate a location. 3. That part of an *instruction* which specifies the location of an *operand* involved in the instruction.

address computation An operation on the *address* part of a *program instruction*.

address, direct Synonymous with *absolute address*.

address format The construction of the *address* part of an *instruction*.

address, machine Synonymous with *absolute address*.

address mapping Conversion of data representing the physical location of *records* and assigning records to *storage locations*, e.g. the translation of a *virtual address* to an *absolute address*.

address modification   The process of changing the *address* part of an *instruction* in such a way that the instruction operates on a different *operand* each time the routine containing the instruction is performed.   ◊ *program modification*.

address part   The part of an *instruction* which contains the *location* of an *operand*.

address register   A *register* in which an *address* is stored.

add-subtract time   The time required to perform one *addition* or *subtraction*, exclusive of the *read time* or *write time*.

add time   The time required to perform one *addition*, exclusive of the *read time* or *write time*.

algebra, Boolean   ◊ *Boolean algebra*.

ALGOL   A *high-level language* used for the presentation to a computer of numerical procedures in a standard form. The word is derived from Algorithmic Oriented Language. The language allows a concise expression of arithmetic and logic processes. ◊ *ALGOL 68*.

ALGOL 68   A powerful *high-level language* designed for use in a number of application areas, and therefore of wider use than, for example, ALGOL 60, the 1960 version of ALGOL. The language ALGOL 68 is more powerful than ALGOL 60, but not an extension of it.

algorithm   A series of instructions or procedural steps designed to result in the solution of a specific problem.

algorithmic   Pertaining to a method of problem-solving by following a predetermined *algorithm*.

allocate   ◊ *storage allocation*.

alphabet   1. Any *character set*, the combinations of which are used to denote data, in accordance with various rules. 2. The character set used in the English language alphabet, often also including symbols such as @, $, £, /.

alphabetic   Pertaining to an *alphabet*. Contrasted with *numeric*.

alphabet code   The representation of data as coded groups of *bits* to represent an *alphabet*[2]. Contrasted with *numeric code*.

alphabetic string   A *string* in which the *characters* are letters, or pertain to an agreed *alphabet* set. Contrasted with *numeric string*.

alphameric   Synonymous with *alphanumeric*.

alphanumeric   Pertaining to a *character set* in which the characters may represent either numerals or letters. Symbols such as @, $,

£, /, may also be represented since these are often included in the term alphabet.

Also known as alphameric.

alteration switch   Synonymous with *indicator*.

alternation   Synonymous with *Or operation*.   ◊ *Boolean algebra*.

alternative denial   Synonymous with *Not-And operation*. ◊ *Boolean algebra*.

ALU   ◊ *arithmetic and logic unit*.

ambiguity error   An error caused as a result of an incorrect selection when there are two possible readings of a digitized number.

amendment record   Synonymous with *change record*.

amplifier   A device which is capable of increasing the magnitude of an effect or action such as an electric wave or a light intensity. Various types of amplifier are used in computing systems, usually accepting an input signal in wave form and delivering a magnified signal. This magnification compensates for *attenuation* introduced by losses inevitable in energy transfer.

amplify   To increase the amplitude of a signal. ◊ *amplifier*.

analog   Pertaining to a device which represents and measures numerical quantities by means of physical variables such as, for example, currents, voltages, mechanical gears. Thus, resistance in an *analog network* can be used to represent mechanical losses and in this way a variable can represent another variable with similar properties.

analog computer   A *computer* which manipulates data by *analog* means. Contrasted with *digital computer*.

analog network   A circuit in which physical variables are represented in such a way that mathematical relationships can be directly indicated by a continuous examination of measurable quantities. The network is usually electrical and serves as a model for a usually non-electrical system.

analog representation   Representation of a variable by a physical quantity (such as voltage), the magnitude of which is directly proportional to the variable.

analog-to-digital conversion   The conversion of *analog* signals to *digital* information by turning physical motion or an electrical voltage into digital factors.

And circuit   Synonymous with *And element*.

And element   A *logical element* operating with *binary digits* which provides one output signal from two input signals in accordance

13

with the following rules:

Input		Output
1	0	0
1	1	1
0	1	0
0	0	0

Also known as And circuit, And gate, coincidence circuit, coincidence element, coincidence gate.

And gate   Synonymous with *And element*.

And operation   A *logical operation*[1] applied to two *operands*. A result is produced depending on the *bit* patterns of the operands and according to the following rules for each *binary digit* position:

Operands		Result
p	q	r
1	0	0
1	1	1
0	1	0
0	0	0

Also known as conjunction, intersection, meet.

annotate   To add explanatory text to *program instructions*. The annotations are often described as narrative.

ANSI   American National Standards Institute. Various ANSI committees have developed standards for computing which have received world-wide acceptance.

anticoincidence element   A *logical element* operating with *binary digits* which provides one output signal from two input signals in accordance with the following rules:

Input		Output
1	0	1
1	1	0
0	1	1
0	0	0

anticoincidence operation   Pertaining to a *logical operation*[1] applied to two *operands*. A result is produced depending on the *bit* patterns of the operands and according to the following rules for each *binary digit* position:

Operands		Result
p	q	r
1	0	1
1	1	0
0	1	1
0	0	0

APL   A *high-level language* with a syntax and character set designed to make it particularly suitable for mathematical applications, especially those involving arrays. The name is derived from A Programming Language.

application   The specific problem to the solution of which data processing techniques are applied. A distinction is often made between applications which are 'computational', i.e. requiring considerable computing capacity, and those which are 'data processing', i.e requiring considerable data handling capacity.

applications package   A *package*[2] designed for an *application*.

applications software   *Programs* and *packages*[2] designed to satisfy *applications*. Contrasted with *systems software.*

architecture   A term beloved of computer manufacturers and used by them to describe the interrelationships between the parts of a computer system.

arithmetic and logic unit   (ALU) The *hardware* unit of a *central*

processor which handles arithmetic and logical operations. ◇
arithmetic unit.

arithmetic check The verification of an arithmetical process by means of a further arithmetical process, e.g. multiplying 22 by 6 and again by 3 to check the result of 18 multiplied by 22.

arithmetic instruction An *instruction* in which the *operator* part specifies an arithmetic operation such as addition, subtraction, multiplication, division, exponentiation. Arithmetic instructions are part of the *function code*, and are distinct from *logical instructions* such as compare, logic sum, logic multiply.

arithmetic operation An operation performed using an *arithmetic instruction.* ◇ *logical operation.*

arithmetic register A *register* constructed to contain the *operands* and results of arithmetic functions on data. Usually part of the *arithmetic unit.*

arithmetic shift A movement of the digits of a number equivalent to a multiplication or division of the number. For example, if a number is stored in *decimal notation* a shift to the right of three places has the effect of dividing by 10^3. Similarly, a shift to the left of two places has the effect of multiplying by 10^2. With numbers stored in *binary notation*, a right shift of n places has the effect of dividing by 2^n and left shift of n places has the effect of multiplying by 2^n.

arithmetic unit The unit which performs arithmetic operations on *operands*. The unit may also be used to perform *arithmetic shifts*, *logical shifts* and other *logical operations* on data.

arm To allow an *interrupt* to occur in accordance with specified priorities. Contrasted with *disarm*.

array An orderly arrangement of items of data, so constructed that the relative position of an element of an array has a relevance to the operation to be performed on that element.

artificial intelligence The ability of any machine or routine to learn and improve its performance as a result of the repeated experience of a given set of problems.

ASCII Acronym for American Standard Code for Information Interchange. A standard code which assigns specific *bit patterns* to the signs, symbols, letters, numbers and operations of a specific set.

assemble To use an *assembler*.

assembler A *program* which turns a *symbolic language* program into a *machine language* program. The program first translates the symbolic operation codes and *addresses* into machine language form; and then groups the resulting machine language program to consolidate library subroutines, program *segments*, adjust *links*, etc. The assembler differs from a *compiler* in that the assembler does not make use of the overall logical structure of the program: the assembler produces machine instructions from the corresponding symbolic instruction on a one-for-one basis without taking account of the context, while a compiler is able to produce a number of machine code instructions from one *pseudo instruction*. The assembler is a translating routine, accepting appropriate subroutines, assembling parts of a routine and making adjustments for links and cross-referencing.

Also known as assembly program, assembly routine.

assembly The process of using an *assembler* to produce a *machine language* program.

assembly language Any *symbolic language* used in connection with a particular *assembler* in order to be converted into *machine language* for use on a computer.

assembly list A list produced during *assembly* to show the details of the *symbolic language* and the corresponding details of the *machine language* created by the *assembler*. The ability to compare the two languages in an assembly list is useful during the *debugging* process.

assembly program Synonymous with *assembler*.

assembly routine Synonymous with *assembler*.

assembly system ◊ *assembler*.

assembly unit Part of a *program* which can be incorporated into a large program by use of an *assembler*, e.g. a *library subroutine*.

assign To reserve a part of a computing system (usually an *input/output* device) for a specific purpose. In *COBOL*, an assignment statement is a procedural statement which associates a *file* with the symbolic name of a device. Contrasted with allocate. ◊ *storage allocation*.

associative storage A storage device in which the *locations* are identified by their contents rather than by their *addresses*, relative positions or symbolic names.

Also known as content addressed storage, parallel search storage and searching storage.

a-stable multivibrator An oscillator capable of generating desired shapes of signals, usually non-sinusoidal shapes. An a-stable multivibrator has a multiplicity of frequencies. ⇔ *flip-flop*, which is a bi-stable multivibrator.

asynchronous working A mode of operation in which the execution of an operation is initiated by a signal generated on completion of the previous operation. This means that the system operates at a speed governed by time constants of the circuitry. Most digital computers have their operations synchronized to a schedule governed by a timing signal or clocking device, and thus operate synchronously rather than asynchronously.

asyndetic Pertaining to the omission of conjunctions or *connectives*.

attach To reserve a system resource such as a *storage* unit for the exclusive use of a specific *program*.

attenuate To cause *attenuation* by a reduction in the amplitude of a signal. Contrasted with *amplify*.

attenuation The reduction in the strength of a signal between transmission and reception.
Also known as loss.

audio Used to describe frequencies capable of being heard by the human ear, i.e. between 15 cycles and 20,000 cycles per second. Some computers use an audio method of indicating that a *program* is completed or a malfunction has occurred, and emit a continuous signal under these circumstances.

audio response unit Pre-recorded responses held in a digitally coded form on a computer *storage device* can be linked by a voice response unit to provide voice responses to input signals.

audit trail The path followed to check that each step in a data processing system may be traced back from machine output to original document. The audit trail begins at the original document but the audit process may start at any point.

augend One of the *operands* employed in *addition*. The quantity to which another quantity (the *addend*) is added, producing a result called the *sum*. The augend is usually replaced by the sum in the addition process.

augment To increase a quantity in order to bring it to a required value.

augmenter A quantity added to another in order to bring it to a required value. It should be noted that an augmenter may be positive or negative.

automatic check A *software* or *hardware* facility for automatically establishing the presence or absence of specific errors.
Also known as built-in check.

automatic coding   Any techniques using a computer to assist in the clerical work of *coding.* ⟡ *relative coding, symbolic language.* Also known as automatic programming.

automatic error correction   A technique which uses *error-detecting codes* and *error-correcting codes.* Errors in transmission are automatically corrected.

automatic interrupt   An interruption to a *program* caused by a *hardware* device or *executive program.* The interruption is caused by an event, independent of the interrupted program. Also known as automatic program interrupt.

automatic program interrupt   Synonymous with *automatic interrupt.*

automatic programming   Synonymous with *automatic coding.*

automatic stop   A *halt programmed* to occur as a result of an error detected by an *automatic check.*

automation   The implementation of a process by automatic means. The field of designing, developing and applying methods and techniques for making machines which are self-actuating and self-controlling.

auxiliary store   Synonymous with *backing store.*

B

babble In *teleprocessing*, the cross-talk from a number of interfering data communications channels.

backgrounding Synonymous with *background processing*.

background processing A phrase to be used with caution as it has directly contradictory meanings, both in common use. 1. Low-priority *tasks*, jobs, *routines*, *subroutines* or *programs* which are executed when a system's resources are not being utilized by higher priority programs. 2. High-priority processing which takes precedence over *foreground processing*. 3. Processing which does not make use of *on-line* facilities.
Also known as backgrounding.

backing storage Synonymous with *backing store*.

backing store Any storage which supports the main *memory* of a *central processor*. Backing store has larger capacity than memory (or immediate access store) and is cheaper, but has slower *access time*.
Also known as auxiliary store, backing storage, bulk storage, bulk store, secondary store.

back mounted A connector mounted from the inside of a box, using mounting flanges placed on the inside of the equipment.

backplane The area into which the *boards* of a system are plugged.
Also known as mother board.

backtracking Processing a list (for example, of names and addresses) in reverse order (for example, reverse alphabetical order).

backward recovery A method of recovering from a system failure by reprocessing *transactions* which have already been applied, thus reconstituting the *file* to an earlier condition.

balanced error An *error range* is said to have a balanced error when all its values have an equal probability and the maximum and minimum values in the range are equal in value and opposite in sign. Contrasted with *bias*[1].

balanced merge sort Synonymous with *balanced sort*.

balanced sort A *merge* sort carried out externally to the *central processor*. Sorted subsets created as a result of internal sorting are equally distributed among half the available *storage devices* and are then merged, using the other available storage devices. The process is repeated until all items are sorted and contained in one set.

Also known as balanced merge sort.

band 1. A group of recording *tracks* on magnetic *storage devices* such as *magnetic drums* and *magnetic disks*. 2. A range of frequencies in the spectrum between two frequency limits. Frequencies are expressed in kiloHertz up to and including 3000 kHz; in megaHertz from there up to and including 3000 MHz; and in gigaHertz up to and including 3000 GHz. Thereafter teraHertz are used.

bandwidth The difference in frequency between the highest and lowest frequency in a *band*[2].

bank ◊ *data bank*.

barrel The cylindrical part of a terminal post that accepts a conductor.

base 1. Synonymous with *radix*. 2. ◊ *data base*. 3. The electrode in a junction transistor lying between the two opposingly *doped* semiconducting media, the collector and emitter.

base address An *address* in a *program instruction* which is the starting point for *program modification*. The base address is used to modify *relative addresses* in order to convert them to *absolute addresses*.

Also known as presumptive address, reference address.

base notation Synonymous with *radix notation*.

base number A quantity which specifies a system of representation for numbers. ◊ *radix notation*.

BASIC A *high-level language* designed for developing *programs* in *conversational mode* in an *on-line* programming environment and consequently popular in universities and for home computers. The name is an acronym for Beginner's All-purpose Symbolic Instruction Code.

basic code Synonymous with *absolute code*.

basic instruction In *program modification* the basic instruction is the instruction which is *modified* in order to obtain the instruction which is to be obeyed.

Also known as presumptive instruction, unmodified instruction.

batch A group of *transactions* collected for processing as a single unit. The transactions may be recorded on original documents or in *machine-readable* form.

batch processing The processing of a *batch*. The implication is that there is a delay between the events which caused the *transactions* in the batch and the processing of these transactions. In a batch processing system the delay is considered acceptable and the cost of providing greater immediacy (such as provided by a *real time* system) has no corresponding benefit.

batch total A total created by the addition of quantities in certain *fields* of a *batch* in order to produce a check that all *records* are available at each stage of processing. The total may be meaningful (e.g. a sum of salaries in a department) or a *hash total* (e.g. a sum of personnel numbers).

baud Named after Baudot, a pioneer of telegraphic communication, a baud is a unit used in measuring the speed of transmission in a telephone or telegraph channel. Originally the unit was equivalent to twice the number of Morse Code dots transmitted continuously per second. When in single-state signalling the modulation rate (expressed in bauds) and the data signalling rate (expressed in *bits* per second) had the same value it was common to use baud as a synonym for bits per second. This does not always apply since with multi-state signalling the modulation rate and data signalling rate cannot have the same value. Bauds should therefore be distinguished from bits per second in describing transmission speed.

BCD Abbreviation for binary coded decimal. ◊ *binary coded decimal notation*.

bead A small *program module* written to perform a specific function. Beads written and tested individually can be strung together and tested in groups known as *threads*.

beam store A magnetic *storage device* in which electron beams are used for the activation or examination of storage cells. A *cathode ray tube* store is a beam store.

beginning-of-file label A *record* at the beginning of a *file*, providing identification of the file and further information about its limits and method of organization.

beginning-of-file section label A *record* at the beginning of a *file* section, providing identification of the section and further information about its limits.

beginning-of-information marker An area of reflective material on a *magnetic tape* indicating the beginning of the recording area.

benchmark A task against which can be measured the performance of a system, *hardware* and *software*. A fixed point of reference from which measurements can be made.

benchmark problem   A problem used as a basis for a *benchmark* in evaluating the performance of computers relative to each other.

bias   1. An *error range* with an average value not equal to zero. Contrasted with *balanced error*. 2. The average DC voltage or current maintained between a control electrode and the common electrode in a transistor.

biconditional operation   Synonymous with *equivalence* operation.

billi-   Prefix denoting 10^9, as in billibit. Synonymous with *giga-*.

binary   A characteristic property involving two possibilities, as in the *binary notation* system in which only the digits 0 and 1 are used.

binary arithmetic operation   Any *arithmetic* operation in which the *operands* are *binary numbers*.

binary Boolean operation   Synonymous with *dyadic Boolean operation*.

binary cell   A storage element capable of storing one *binary digit*, i.e. a zero or a one.

binary chain   A series of *binary* circuits arranged so that each circuit can affect the next circuit.

binary chop   A method of searching a *table* ordered in a known sequence by comparing the required *key* with a key half-way in the table. If the comparison shows that the required key is in the top half of the table, the bottom half is rejected and a key half-way in the top half is examined. The process is repeated, dividing the remainder of the table in half until the required key is found. Also known as binary search, dichotomizing search.

binary code   A code in which *numeric* and *alphabetic characters* (or *symbols*) are represented by groups of *binary digits*.

binary coded character   A character represented by a *binary code*.

binary coded decimal notation   A method of representing decimal numbers by groups of *binary digits*, with each *digit position* of a decimal number being allocated four *bits*. (Note that each decimal digit is separately coded.)

binary coded decimal representation   ◊ *binary coded decimal notation*.

binary coded digit   Any numeral represented by a coded group of *binary digits*. For example, the use of four *bits* to represent a decimal digit, or the use of three bits to represent a digit in the *octal* scale of notation.

binary digit   A digit in the *binary* scale of notation; i.e. either 1 or 0. Generally abbreviated as *bit*.

binary half adder   A *half adder* operating with digits representing binary signals, capable of receiving two inputs and of delivering two outputs, as follows:

Input		Output	
Augend	*Addend*	*Sum*	*Carry*
1	0	1	0
1	1	0	1
0	1	1	0
0	0	0	0

binary notation   A system of representing numbers in which the *radix* for each *digit position* is two. Numbers are represented by the digits 0 and 1 and displacement of one digit position to the left means multiplication by two. Thus the binary number '10' represents two, while '1000' represents eight.

binary number   A number represented in *binary notation*. ⟡ *binary numeral*.

binary numeral   One of the two digits 0 and 1 used for representing numbers in *binary notation*. ⟡ *binary number*.

binary operation   1. Any operation using two *operands*; a dyadic operation. 2. Any operation involving the use of operands in binary form – a *binary arithmetic operation*.

binary pair   Synonymous with *flip-flop*.

binary point   A point which separates the integral from the fractional part of a *binary number*, performing the same function in the *binary notation* system as the decimal point performs in the decimal system.

binary representation   ⟡ *binary notation*.

binary search   Synonymous with *binary chop*.

binary-to-decimal conversion   Conversion of a number represented in *binary notation* to the equivalent in decimal notation. A change in the recording medium is often involved in such a conversion: for example, the binary number may be stored in main *memory*, and the decimal number may appear on a *terminal screen*.

binary variable   A *variable* which can have one of two values, 0 or 1.

Also known as two-valued variable.

bind   To transform one or more *object code program modules* into a program suitable for *execution*.

bipolar   An input signal is bipolar if signals of different electrical voltage polarity represent different logical states. Contrasted with *unipolar*.

biquinary code   A number representation system in which each decimal digit (n) is represented by a pair of numbers (x, y) where $n = x + y$ and $x = 0$ or 5, $y = 0$, 1, 2, 3 or 4. The following table shows decimal and biquinary representation of each digit, and also a binary representation of the pair.

Decimal	Biquinary	Binary representation
0	0 + 0	0 000
1	0 + 1	0 001
2	0 + 2	0 010
3	0 + 3	0 011
4	0 + 4	0 100
5	5 + 0	1 000
6	5 + 1	1 001
7	5 + 2	1 010
8	5 + 3	1 011
9	5 + 4	1 100

bistable   Pertaining to the ability of a device to assume either of two stable states at any particular instant. ⇨ *flip-flop*.

bistable circuit   Synonymous with *flip-flop*.

bistable multivibrator   Synonymous with *flip-flop*.

bit   A contraction of *binary digit*. One of the two characters (0 and 1) used in *binary notation*. Also signifies the smallest unit of data, and is often used to mean the physical representation of a binary digit, e.g. as a magnetized spot on a recording surface or a pulse in an electronic circuit.

bit, check   A binary digit used as a *check digit*.

bit density   The number of *bits* stored in a *storage* area.

bite   Alternative spelling for *byte*.

bit location   An element of *store* able to store one *bit*.

bit pattern   A representation of *characters* in a *binary code*.

bit position   A *word* has a number of *digit positions* and each is known as a bit position, referenced as the first, second, third, etc, from the least significant position.

bit rate   The speed at which *bits* can be transferred over a communications channel. May be measured in bits per second or in *bauds*.

bit, sign   ◊ *sign bit.*

bit-slice   ◊ *bit-slice microprocessor.*

bit-slice microprocessor   *Microprocessors* of, for example, two- or four-*bit word* length, chained together and *microprogrammed* to form processors of longer word length. Each bit-slice performs a specific function within the chain.

bit string   A sequence of *binary digits* representing data in coded form. Each *bit* has significance according to its position in the *string* and its relation to other members of that string.

bit track   A physical track on a *magnetic disk* or *drum* along which *bits* are recorded or read by a *read/write head*. Compare with *logical track.*

black box approach   Acceptance of computed results without feeling the need to question the method of working of the computer.

blank   1. A part of a data medium in which data is not recorded. But ◊ *blank character.* 2. To make a display blank by switching off a *terminal screen*, or by not displaying any *characters*.

blank character   A *character* used to represent a space (i.e. a separation between groups of characters) and sometimes in itself acting as an instruction for further action. A blank character is not necessarily an empty position on a recording medium, and may have a specific *bit pattern* like any other character.
Also known as space character.

blank instruction   Synonymous with *do-nothing instruction.*

blast   1. To release external or internal *memory* area under *dynamic storage allocation*. 2. Synonymous with *blow.*

blind   To make a device incapable of receiving certain types of data.

b-line   Synonymous with *index register.*

blip   1. In graphics, a document mark. 2. An erratic signal on a *terminal screen.*

block   A group of *records* or *words* treated as a logical unit of data; e.g. data is moved between *memory* and *peripheral units* in blocks rather than record by record. Blocks may be fixed in length or of variable size.

block copy To *copy* a *file* without changing its contents, particularly to copy a file from one medium to another. ⟐ *block transfer*.

block diagram The diagrammatic representation of any system (e.g. a computer *program*, an electrical circuit) in which logical units of the system are represented by annotated boxes and the relationship between units is shown by interconnecting lines. The block diagram is concerned more with the functioning and relationships of major parts of a system than with the precise details of these parts, and is coarser than a *flowchart*.

blockette A subdivision of a *block* which is *input*[1] and *output*[2] as a single unit or block in its own right.

block header Data at the beginning of a *block* describing the organization of the *file* and the relationship between blocks.

block ignore character A *character* indicating that the *block* relating to the character is to be ignored during processing as it contains at least one error created during data input.

blocking The creation of *blocks* from individual *records*.

blocking factor The maximum number of *records* of a given size which can be grouped into a single *block*.

block length The size of a *block*, measured in the number of *words*, *records* or *characters* it contains.

block list A *printout* of the contents of a *file* in which *records* are listed in the sequence in which they appear with the minimum reformatting. The printout is then used for identifying data errors.

block mark A *character* used to indicate the end of a *block* in systems in which variable-length blocks are used.

block, output ⟐ *output block*.

block transfer The movement of data (e.g. between a *central processor* and a *peripheral unit*) as *blocks* rather than as *records*.

blow The process of writing into a *programmable read-only memory* (PROM), or variants such as *EPROM*. Contrasted with *zap*. Also known as blast, burn.

blowback An image enlargement on a *cathode ray tube*.

blue ribbon program A *program* which runs successfully at the first attempt.
Also known as star program.

board A rectangular sheet on which integrated circuits are mounted; boards are themselves then mounted on a *chassis*. ⟐ *circuit board*.

Boolean algebra A system of using algebraic notation to express logical relationships, just as conventional algebra is used to express mathematical relationships. In Boolean algebra (named after the mathematician George Boole, 1815–64) the variables of an expression do not represent numbers but statements and the logical operations which relate them such as 'Or', 'And', 'Nor'. In a simplification of Boolean algebra the values of the variables are limited to two values (known as *truth values*) 'true' and 'false'. The *binary* logic of computers can thus be readily related to the logic of Boolean algebra, and computers can follow different instructions depending on the result of a comparison of data. Circuits designed to simulate the Boolean operations are known as *logical elements*.

Also known as Boolean calculus, Boolean logic.

Boolean calculus   Synonymous with *Boolean algebra*.

Boolean connective   A symbol used to connect the *operands* in a statement of a *Boolean operation*. The connective shows which type of operation is concerned.

Boolean logic   Synonymous with *Boolean algebra*.

Boolean operation   A *logical operation*[1] which depends on the rules of *Boolean algebra*. A Boolean operation may involve any number of *operands*.

Boolean operation, dyadic   ◊ *dyadic Boolean operation*.

Boolean operation table   An operation table designed to show how each of a set of *operands* and results assumes one of two values.

boot   A protective housing preventing moisture from entering into a connector.

bootstrap   A procedure for initiating the *loading* of a *program* into a computer as a result of preliminary *instructions*. These first instructions are usually called into action by the use of a *console* switch or message from the console, and once they have been initiated they call other instructions to read programs and data.

bounceless contact   A mechanical contact that has been conditioned by means of a *flip-flop* or a device with only one stable state to eliminate all noise during contact.

box   A symbol (often a rectangle) used to represent a logical unit of a system or *program* in a *block diagram* or *flowchart*. But ◊ *decision box*.

branch   To select, as a result of a *decision*, one of a number of sets of *instructions* in a *program*. A branch is a sequence of instructions lying between two *branch instructions*.

Also known as jump.

branching   ◊ *branch* and *branch instruction*.

branch instruction An *instruction* which specifies the *address* of the next instruction, depending on the result of an arithmetic or *logical operation* or on the state of an indicator or *switch*. A branch instruction may be conditional or unconditional.

Also known as control transfer instruction, discrimination instruction, jump instruction.

branchpoint The point in a *program* where a *branch* takes place.

breadboard A roughly made experimental model of a device used to test the design parameters.

break To interrupt a user sending on a communication channel in order to take control of the channel.

breakpoint A point in a *program* specified by an *instruction* where the normal sequence of operations may be interrupted by external intervention (e.g. by an operator signal or by a *monitor routine* used in *debugging*). The normal sequence is resumed after the interruptions, which will have been used for a visual check or a display on a *terminal*, for example.

breakpoint halt Synonymous with *breakpoint instruction*.

breakpoint instruction A *program instruction* placed at a *breakpoint* to cause the program to transfer control to a *monitor routine* in *debugging* operations or to take other special action after an external interruption such as a signal from an operator's *console*.

Also known as breakpoint halt.

breakpoint symbol A symbol included in an *instruction* to indicate that there is a *breakpoint* at this instruction.

b-register Synonymous with *index register*.

bridgeware Transition aids, *hardware* or *software*, used in transcribing *programs* and *data files* written for one type of computer into the format appropriate for another type of computer.

bridging Using *bridgeware* to convert systems from a format and structure suitable for one type of computer to a format and structure suitable for another.

b-store Synonymous with *index register*.

bubble memory In a single crystal sheet minute cylinders with axes lying perpendicular to the sheet can be magnetized and, since the presence or absence of a magnetized cylinder, or bubble, can represent binary data, the bubbles can provide *memory*. Advantages include non-volatility, low power consumption and very high *packing density*.

bucket In *random-access memory*, a place or unit of storage. A place where data may be stored, as distinct from the data contained. The data is accessed by reference to the bucket in which it is located.

buffer A store which is designed to compensate for the different data rate between a transmitting device and a receiving device. A temporary store, e.g. between a *central processor* and a *peripheral unit*. A buffer may be a permanent feature of a device, or may be a temporarily assigned area of *memory*.
Also known as buffer store.

buffer computer A computer in which *buffers* are provided to compensate for the difference between the speed of the peripheral units and the higher speed of the *central processor*.

buffered input/output The use of *input/output buffers* to increase efficiency when data is transmitted to and from a *central processor*.

buffering The management of *buffers*. ⊗ *dynamic buffering*, *exchange buffering*, *simple buffering*.

buffer store Synonymous with *buffer*.

bug Any defect or malfunction of a computer, *program*, or system. Bugs are identified as a result of *diagnostic routines* and test routines. They are then exterminated, but execution is not always immediate.

built-in check Synonymous with *automatic check* or (when applied only to *hardware*) *hardware check*.

bulk storage Synonymous with *backing store*.

bulk store Synonymous with *backing store*.

burn Synonymous with *blow*.

burst 1. A set of *characters* grouped together for data transmission. An interval occurs between bursts to allow access to the store from which the bursts are being transmitted. 2. To separate sheets of a continuous form along its perforations.

burst mode Data transfer between *central processor* and *peripheral units* in *bursts*.

bus A conductor used for transmitting signals from one or more sources to one or more destinations. A single wire serving one source and one destination is not generally considered to be a bus, and usually a number of connections are made to a common bus for the use of many circuits.
Also known as highway, trunk.

bus driver A power *amplifier* used to drive *logic elements* by means of a conductor or *bus*.
Also known as line driver.

byte   A group of adjacent *binary digits* operated on as one unit; usually a subdivision of a *word*.

byte mode   A method of transfer of data between a *central processor* and a *peripheral unit* in which the unit of transfer is a single *byte*.

C

CAD   Abbreviation for computer aided design.

CAI   Abbreviation for computer assisted instruction.

call   1. To transfer control in a *program* by means of a *branch* to a *subroutine*. 2. In communications, to make use of a connection between two stations.

calling sequence   A group of *program instructions* and data arranged to set up and *call*[1] a specific *subroutine*. When control has been transferred to the subroutine a further group of instructions is necessary to provide a link back to the main program, and this link is also known as a calling sequence.

capacitance   A measure of the ability to store electric charge, the basic unit of measurement being a *farad*.

capacitor   An electronic device with the properties of *capacitance*.

capacity   1. The number of units of storage (*words*, *bytes* or *characters*) that a *storage device* is capable of holding. 2. The length of a *register*, expressed as a number of digits or characters.

capstan   The shaft on a magnetic *tape deck* on which a reel of *magnetic tape* is mounted.

card   1. ◊ *punched card*. 2. ◊ *circuit board*.

card cage   A frame or chassis for holding a *central processor*, *memory cards*[2] and *interfaces*.
Also known as card chassis.

card chassis   Synonymous with *card cage*.

card code   A combination of holes in a *punched card* representing letters of the alphabet, numerals or special symbols.

card format   A representation of the columns and *fields* of data in a *punched card*.

card image   An exact representation in *store* of each hole in a *punched card*. More usually, it is the character represented by a combination of holes which is represented in store.

card loader   A routine used to load a *program* from *punched cards* into *store*.

carousel   A rotary device which presents a data medium such as film or microfilm at an identified position for reading or recording.

carriage tape   Synonymous with *control tape*.

carrier frequency The frequency of an unmodulated carrier wave subject to modulation for the representation of data.

carrier system A system which allows a number of independent communications signals to share a single path. Each *channel* signal is allowed to modulate one carrier at a different frequency, and at the receiving end the *demodulator* separates the signals by selective tuning.

carry An overflow from a single digit column, after an *addition* operation. When the sum of two or more digits in a digit position exceeds the *radix*, the digit added to the next higher digit position is known as the carry.

carry-complete signal A signal from an *adder* indicating that all *carries* relevant to an operation have been made.

carry time The time taken in transferring a *carry* digit to its next higher digit position.

cartridge A unit of *storage*, containing data or *programs*, which may be easily inserted into or removed from a drive-control unit. The implication of the word is that the unit is comparatively small, both in terms of storage capacity and handling capability.

cascade control A system of organizing control units in sequence so that each unit regulates the operation of its successor and is in turn regulated by its predecessor.

cascaded carry A *carry* into a digit position resulting in an immediate carry out of the same digit position. A cascaded carry is due only to a carry from a previous position and does not result from digits already in a column. Usually a carry is said to be cascaded when the normal adding circuits are used to handle it, rather than special *high-speed carry* circuits set up to handle such a carry.

cassette tape *Backing store magnetic tape* driven in a cassette rather than a large-scale *tape deck*.

casting-out-nines A check on an arithmetic operation, using a remainder obtained from the *operand* by dividing by nine and carrying out the same operations on the remainders as are performed on the operands.

CAT Abbreviation for computer assisted training.

catalanguage Synonymous with *object language*.

catalogue A list of objects (*files*, devices, *program* names, users) used or handled within a system, arranged in an order which allows easy location.

catena 1. A series of items linked together in a *chained list*. 2. Specifically, a *string* of *characters* in a *word*.

catenate To arrange a series of items in a *catena*. Also known as concatenate.

cathode follower An electronic circuit. A form of *buffer amplifier* in which a thermionic valve is used, and in which the potential of the cathode follows that of the grid with little or no phase shift.

cathode ray tube (CRT) A device consisting of a vacuum tube, a display screen, and a beam of electrons controlled and directed by deflection. The device may be used as a display or a storage device or both.

cathode ray tube storage Synonymous with *electrostatic storage*.

CCD Abbreviation for *charge couple device*.

Ceefax A broadcast television screen message service, allowing a modified domestic television receiver to accept text messages. ⇔ *Oracle, Prestel, viewdata*.

cell ⇔ *binary cell*.

cellar Synonymous with *pushdown store*.

central processing unit (CPU) Synonymous with *central processor*.

central processor If the six basic parts of a computer system are internal storage (*memory*), *control unit, arithmetic unit, input, output* and *external store*, then the central processor contains the first three. It is usual to think of a *microprocessor* as containing these three while a *microcomputer* also includes *interfaces* to the remaining three parts. In large *data processing* systems the central processor is often referred to as the *main frame*, but the word is also used to distinguish between such large systems and *minicomputer* systems and microprocessors. Also known as central processing unit, processor.

chad The piece of material removed when a code hole or notch is punched in *paper tape* or a *punched card*.

chadded tape 1. *Paper tape* punched so that the *chads* are completely removed, thus making complete chads. 2. Paper tape punched so that the chads are only partially removed, thus making the chads still attached. Since these two definitions are quite contradictory they should be used with caution. Use of the phrase *chadless tape* provides no greater safety.

chadless tape 1. *Paper tape* punched so that the *chads* are completely removed, thus rendering the tape without chads. 2. Paper tape punched so that the chads are only partially removed, thus making tape without complete chads. For comments on the contrariness of these definitions ⇔ *chadded tape*.

chain 1. A series of data items joined by references such as the *address* of the next data item. 2. A number of *segments* linked together by the fact that each segment uses as input the output of the previous segment. 3. A set of items arranged as a *chained list*. ⇔ *catena*, *binary chain*, *Markov chain*.

chain code A grouping of *words* in which adjacent words are linked in such a way that each word is derived from the preceding word by displacing the *bits* one digit position left or right, dropping the leading bit and inserting the next bit at the end. The inserted bit must satisfy the requirement that a word must not recur until the cycle is complete.

chained file A *file* of data organized so that each unit of data has an *address* of another unit which contains the same *data element*. Therefore all *records* containing a given data element can be retrieved once the first such record has been found.
Also known as threaded file.

chained list Data arranged in such a way that each item contains an *address* to identify the next item in the set. The items may therefore be scattered throughout a file.

chained record A record in a *chained file*. The first record to be found is a *home record*.

chaining search A method of searching a set of data organized as a *chain*.

chain printer A high-speed printer in which the type is carried on a moving closed loop chain or belt past the paper, with each character printing in the required position as a result of being struck by an appropriate hammer.

change dump A selective *printout* or other output of all *storage locations* whose contents have changed since a previous event (usually another change dump).

change file A file of *transactions* forming *change records*. The file is used to *update* a *master file* during *batch processing*.
Also known as detail file, transaction file.

change record A *record* which contains fresh information and the function of which is to *update* a corresponding *master record*.
Also known as amendment record, transaction record.

change tape Synonymous with *transaction tape*.

channel A physical path along which data may be transmitted or stored.

channel, peripheral interface ⟡ *interface*.

channel queue 1. A queue of data waiting to be processed on a *channel*. 2. A queue of requests for the use of a channel.

channel status table A *table* maintained by an *executive program* to indicate the status of the various *peripheral interface channels*.

channel-to-channel connection Connection of appropriate *channels* of two or more computer systems to allow the transfer of data between computers.

chapter Synonymous with *segment*.

character A mark or event forming one of a set of marks or events and used to denote, for example, the numbers 0–9, the letters of the alphabet, punctuation marks, etc.

character blink A feature on a *terminal* device which allows one or more *characters* to blink in unison with the main *cursor* or out of synchronization with the main cursor. Some terminals allow whole words, paragraphs or columns to blink.

character check A check that makes sure that character format rules have been followed.

character code A code used to represent a *character* in a computer system; a combination of elements such as *bits* to do this.

character crowding A reduction of the appropriate interval between *characters* on a magnetic medium. ⟡ *pack*.

character density The number of *characters* stored in a unit of length, area or volume. ⟡ *packing density*.

character fill To insert into a *storage* medium a representation of a specified *character*, usually in order to *overwrite* unwanted data and indicate an error condition.

characteristic The part of a *floating-point number* which indicates the exponent.

characteristic overflow The result of an attempt to create a *characteristic* greater than the specified upper limit.

characteristic underflow The result of an attempt to create a *characteristic* less than the specified lower limit.

character modifier A constant used in *address modification* to reference the *location* of a *character*.

character oriented Pertaining to a computer in which *character locations* rather than *words* are *addressed*.

character reader A device capable of converting printed characters into electrical pulses which can be recognized by a *central processor*.

character recognition The identification of *characters*, with the implication of doing so by automatic means, e.g. *magnetic ink character recognition*, *optical character recognition*.

character, redundant ◊ *check character*. The word redundant in microprocessor vocabulary is often used with the implication 'extra' or 'held in reserve' rather than 'surplus to requirement'. ◊ *redundancy*.

character repertoire The set of *characters* available in a particular code. Related to *character set*.

character set The group of *characters* which together form a recognizable code accepted as valid by a specific computer. A character set is not necessarily an ordered, sequential set. (Contrasted with *alphabet*, for example, which is ordered.)

character string A one-dimensional array of characters held either in *memory* or in another storage medium.

character subset A selection of characters from a *character set*; e.g. the subset that includes alphabetic characters only. (The alphabetic subset is not necessarily in order.)

charge couple device (CCD) A *memory* device with high *packing density* and low power consumption. Chains of potential wells couple and allow charges to move smoothly from one well to another, giving a precise period of delay during the ripple process. Also known as image sensor.

chart A diagrammatic representation of a data processing problem or solution. ◊ *block diagram*, *flowchart*.

chassis A frame on which *boards* are mounted. But ◊ *hot chassis*.

check Any operation designed to determine accuracy or validity. A check may, for example, test for the absence of error in a set of data, or may test for whether certain prescribed conditions have been met.

check bit A binary *check digit*.

check character A *character* which has no data function but whose purpose is to act as a check on other characters in the same group. Its value is dependent on the values of the other characters in the group and the check takes place when the group is stored or transferred.

check digit A digit which has no data function but which is carried with a group of digits and varies in value as the values of the other digits in the group change. The check digit allows the detection of inaccurate transfer, storage or retrieval in subsequent stages of processing.
Also known as check number.

check indicator An indicator, either *hardware* or *software*, which shows that a check has failed. A hardware indicator might cause, for example, a *console* display or an internal switch to be set. A software indicator might result in the printing of an error message.

check number Synonymous with *check digit*.

checking program A *program* which diagnoses format, syntax and coding errors in other programs.
Also known as checking routine.

checking routine Synonymous with *checking program*.

check number Synonymous with *check digit*.

checkout To apply diagnostic or test procedures to a *program* or to a computer system.

checkout routine Synonymous with *debugging aid routine*.

checkpoint A point in a *program* at which data and results from computations are *stored*, thus making it a suitable departure point for *restarting* if this should become necessary.

checkpoint dump To record data at a *checkpoint*.

check problem A test problem with a known solution. If the problem is incorrectly solved, a *program* or computer *error* condition is indicated.

check register A *register* in which data is stored temporarily before a comparison is made with the same data input at a different time or by a different path.

check sum A summation of individual digits in a number according to an arbitrary set of rules. The result is not meaningful but is used as part of a checking process. Sometimes used as a synonym for *hash total*.

check total Synonymous with *control total*.

Cheshire Cat store Synonymous with *regenerative memory*.

chip A single device consisting of transistors, diodes and other components forming the essential elements of a *central processor* on a section of a *wafer* sliced from a crystal of silicon.

chopper A device which interrupts a current or a beam of light to produce a pulsating signal.

chopper-stabilized amplifier A device to stabilize fluctuations in a circuit. A modulator in the device acts as a *chopper*.

circuit A closed-loop path along which electric current can flow.

circuit board A board to which is attached the circuitry of a microprocessor. A number of circuit boards can be slotted in to a *card cage* or *mother board*.
Also known as card, circuit card.

circuit card   Synonymous with *circuit board*.

circuit noise level   The amount of disturbance in a *data transmission* circuit.

circular list   A *chained list*, which, after processing all items from any starting point, allows return to the item preceding the starting point.

circular shift   Synonymous with *cyclic shift*.

circulating register   A *register* in which the digits can be moved out of one end and re-entered at the other end, as if they were in a *closed loop*.

circulating storage   Synonymous with *dynamic store*.

clamp   A circuit which ensures that the electrical potential of one point does not exceed a certain value. A clamp in a computer logic circuit is designed to hold a particular part of a waveform at a specified voltage level.

clamp-on   To hold a telephone call while waiting for a line which is in use.

classical   ⋄ *conventional*.

clear   To place every *location* in a *storage device* into the same state, usually zero or blank.

clear area   Synonymous with *clear band*.

clear band   In *optical character recognition*, a specified area on a document which must be kept free of printing.
Also known as clear area.

clock   A device capable of generating signals at periodic intervals. In digital *synchronous* computers the generation of pulses is controlled by clocks and these pulses govern the timing of events such as the inhibiting or enabling of *gates*.

clock pulse   A pulse emitted by a *clock* to synchronize operations carried out by a digital *synchronous* computer.

clock rate   The frequency at which pulses are emitted from a *clock*.

clock track   A *track* on a magnetic recording medium on which a continuous string of pulses is recorded to provide a signal to control *read* and *write* operations.

close   To *call* a *subroutine* to end the reading from or writing to a *file* by a *program*.

closed array   An *array* that cannot be extended because any addition would change the value of the entire array.

closed loop   1. A *program loop* with no exit. The *execution* of such a loop can be interrupted only by operator intervention, or by action from an *executive program* monitoring the performance of the program containing the loop. 2. A system in which the output is fed back to adjust the input. Synonymous with *feedback*.

closed shop A computer installation from which programming staff are excluded while their *programs* are being run. It is felt that this exclusion minimizes the time spent in *debugging* and ensures that considerable care is taken in checking programs before they are presented.

Also known as hands-off operation.

closed subroutine A *subroutine* in which a re-entry point for returning to the main *routine* is generated in accordance with conditions established on entry to the subroutine. Contrasted with *open subroutine*.

Also known as linked subroutine.

cluster 1. A group of *drive* units for magnetic medium devices. 2. A group of related documents in a document retrieval system.

CMOS Complementary metal oxide *semiconductor* technology, using both n-channel and p-channel devices (⬦ *n-type* and *p-type*) on the same silicon *substrate*.

coalesce To combine two or more sets of *files*.

COBOL A *high-level language* designed to allow the expression of data manipulation and business data processing problems in a form of recognizable English narrative. The word is derived from Common Business Oriented Language.

CODASYL Conference on Date System Languages, a committee brought into being by the United States Department of Defense. The Committee developed specifications for COBOL and has a powerful influence on the design and acceptance of other languages.

code 1. The set of rules used for converting data from one representation to another. 2. The representation of data or *instructions* in symbolic form. 3. To convert data or instructions into such a form.

code area 1. An area of *main memory* containing *program instructions* rather than data. 2. The area of a microfilm frame used for storing a retrieval code.

code, computer Synonymous with *machine code*.

code, cyclic Synonymous with *Gray code*.

coded decimal notation Synonymous with *binary coded decimal notation*.

code, direct Synonymous with *absolute code*.

code-directing characters   *Characters* used to indicate the routing and destination of the message to which they are attached.

coded stop   Synonymous with *programmed halt*.

code element   One of the discrete conditions of a code; for example, the presence or absence of a pulse in a *binary code*, or a dot or a dash in the Morse code.

code frame   A group of *characters* which recurs cyclically.

code line   The written form of a *program instruction*.

code, macro   Synonymous with *macroinstruction*.

code, minimum delay   Synonymous with *minimum access code*.

code, minimum latency   Synonymous with *minimum access code*.

code, one-level   Synonymous with *absolute code*.

code, optimum   Synonymous with *minimum access code*.

code position   The locations in a data recording medium where data may be entered, e.g. a character printed or a hole punched.

coder   A somewhat derogatory term for a *programmer*[1], with the implication that a coder is able only to write *instructions* from *flowcharts* prepared by someone else, while a programmer is also capable of preparing the flowcharts.

code, self-checking   Synonymous with *error-detecting code*.

code, single-address   Synonymous with *single-address instruction*.

code, specific   Synonymous with *absolute code*.

code, symbolic   Synonymous with *symbolic instruction*.

code transparent   Pertaining to the ability to transmit *characters* regardless of their *binary code*.

coding   The writing of *instructions* for a computer. *Programming* embraces coding. ⊄ *coder*.

coding check   A test carried out to establish that a *program* is error-free. An initial coding check is usually made by working through the program on paper. ⊄ *dry run*.

coding sheet   A pre-printed form on which *program instructions* are written. The grid-like format ensures that transcription to an input medium is carried out with the minimum number of errors.

coding, specific   ⟁ *absolute code*.

coefficient   Synonymous with *fixed-point part*.

coincidence circuit   Synonymous with *And element*.

coincidence element   Synonymous with *And element*.

coincidence gate   Synonymous with *And element*.

cold fault   A computer fault which is apparent as soon as the machine is switched on.

collate To produce one ordered set of items from two or more sets which are in the same ordered sequence. Synonymous with *merge*.

collator 1. A *program* which *collates* sets of data. 2. A *punched card* device which collates sets of cards.

collector 1. The electrode in a point-contact transistor or the area in a junction transistor to which electrons or ions migrate under the influence of an electrical field. 2. A *software module* used in *compiling* to *collate program* modules into a form suitable for *loading*.

column binary A *punched card* representation of a series of *binary digits* by the presence or absence of holes in successive columns of the card.

COM Acronym for computer output on microfilm. Computer *printout* is converted to positive film, with one piece of film containing many greatly reduced pages. COM readers allow a selected part of the film to be magnified *off-line* and if required a copy is produced of the document in its original size.

combinational circuit A logic device which has no storage capability and whose output values at any instant depend on the input values at that instant.

combined head Synonymous with *read/write head*.

combined read/write head Synonymous with *read/write head*.

command Synonymous with *instruction*.

command chain A sequence of *input/output instructions* which can be *executed* independently of the process of which they form a part.

command language A *source language* consisting mainly of *instructions* capable of specifying a function.

comment Written notes which are included in the *coding* of *instructions* in order to clarify the purpose of the instruction or group of instructions to which the notes relate. The comment has no effect on the operation of the program itself; it is included in the *source language* but is not translated into *machine language*. Also known as narrative.

commission To instal a computer and ensure that it is capable of successful operation. Commissioning is sometimes taken to include an *acceptance test* and sometimes taken to precede it.

common area An area of *store* which can be used by more than one *program*, or by more than one *segment* or *routine* of one program. ⟡ *multiprogramming* and *overlay*.
Also known as common storage area.

Common Business Oriented Language ◊ *COBOL*.

common hardware Items, usually expendable, which have many possible applications and are held as stocks for repair. Typical items are nuts, bolts, screws and plugs. Contrasted with *common software*.

common language The representation of data in a form intelligible to other units in a data processing system, so that information can be readily transferred between parts of the system.

common software Software items such as *subroutines* which have many possible applications in many systems written in the same *language*.

common storage area Synonymous with *common area*.

common target machine ◊ *target computer*.

communication channel Any channel for enabling a *communications* link.

communication link Synonymous with *data link*.

communications The process of transmitting and receiving data, sometimes including the process of validation. Communications devices make use of telephones, satellites and any means of sending digital signals.

communications link controller An *interface* device between a computer and a *communications* network.

commutator pulse A pulse issued at a particular instant to define a particular *binary digit* in a *word*, setting the limits of a *digit period*.
Also known as p-pulse, position pulse.

compaction The use of one or other of the techniques available for making better use of space in *memory* by *packing* data.

comparator A device for determining whether there is any difference between two items and producing a signal dependent on the result of the comparison. The process may be carried out to compare two different items or two versions of the same item in order to test the accuracy of data transfer.
Also known as comparing unit.

compare To examine the relationship between two data items, and to signal the result. The comparison may take place in a *comparator* and can result in any one of the possibilities 'equal to', 'greater than', or 'less than'. The result may be signalled by setting an *indicator*, or by a *conditional branch instruction*.

comparing unit Synonymous with *comparator*.

compatible Two computers are said to be compatible if *programs* can be successfully run on them without alteration. They may be two computers of the same type but different *configuration* or two computers of different types. If a program written for one can be run on the second, but one written for the second cannot be run on the first (because it makes use of facilities or features not contained in the first) then the computers are said to be upwards compatible.

compile   To prepare a *machine language program* from a program written in a *source language* by means of a *compiler*[1].

compile-and-go   Pertaining to an operating technique in which there are no intermediate steps between the *compiling*, *loading* and *execution* of a *program*.

compile phase   The part of a *run* which includes the *execution* of a *compiler*.

compiler   1. A program which prepares a *machine language* program from *instructions* written in a *source language*. The program is more complex than an *assembler* (to which in many respects it is similar) because (a) the symbolic language instruction is not translatable on a one-for-one basis into machine code, (b) *library subroutines* can be called and the compiler will incorporate them into the *object program*, (c) interconnecting links between different parts of the program are supplied by the compiler. 2. A harmless drudge.

compiler diagnostics   Facilities in a *compiler*[1] which detect syntactical errors in *source programs* and produce listings in the source language and *machine code*, accompanied by *error messages*.

compiler interface   Functions carried out by an *operating system* to provide supporting capability to a *compiler*[1].

compiler manager   *Software*, usually part of an *operating system*, which controls the process of *compiling*.

complement   A numeral derived from another in accordance with one or more specified rules: the type of complement is determined by the rule, and a complement does not exist until the rule is stated and applied. In many computers a negative number is represented as the complement of the corresponding positive number. There are two common rules: (a) subtract each digit from one less than the *radix* and add one to the result; this is known as the radix complement, noughts complement or true complement. (b) As for (a) but without adding one to the result; this is known as the diminished radix complement, radix-minus-one complement or – in decimal – nines complement, and – in binary – ones complement.

complementary operation A *Boolean operation* which results in the negation of another Boolean operation. For example, Nand is complementary to And.

complementing Carrying out a *complementary operation*.

complete carry The result when a *carry* which arises from the addition of carries is allowed to propagate a carry.

complete operation The implementation of an *instruction*, including the obtaining of the instruction, interpreting it, obtaining the associated *operands*, executing the instruction and placing the results in *store*.

compound statement Two or more *statements* which may be *executed* at *run time* as a single statement.

compute mode In an *analog computer* the operating mode in which input signals are directly connected to computing units.

computer A device capable of accepting data, solving problems and supplying the results; usually assumed to have an *input* unit, a store or *memory* unit, an *arithmetic and logic unit*, a *control unit*, and an *output* unit. Computers are further distinguished as *main frame computers*, *minicomputers* and, curiously, *microprocessors*. (It is proper to distinguish between a microprocessor and a microcomputer by recognizing that the latter includes peripheral *interfaces* and *storage*; but this is seldom done, and microprocessor tends to embrace microcomputer.) ⬦ *analog computer*, *digital computer*.

computer, analogue ⬦ *analog computer*.

computer applications A general term for the uses to which a computer may be put. Applications software is distinguished from *systems software*. ⬦ *applications package*.

computer code Synonymous with *machine code*.

computer instruction ⬦ *instruction*.

computer program ⬦ *program*.

computer system 1. The *hardware* of a *central processor* and associated *peripheral units*, including *systems software*. 2. The *application* of computers to the solution of a problem; including hardware, systems software and applications software.

computing amplifier An amplifier in which the output voltage is related by *negative feedback* to the input voltage.
Also known as operational amplifier.

concatenate Synonymous with *catenate*.

concentrator A *multiplexor* connected to more communications channels than it can handle at one time, so that it cannot handle *contention*[2]. For example, in a switched telephone network the system is so configured that it is not possible for all subscribers to access each other at the same time, although no subscriber feels constrained from attempting an access. Note that if accesses are operating under computer control the device is a *front-end processor*, not a concentrator.

concurrent conversion The simultaneous running of *conversion programs* with other programs. ⟨⟩ *multiprogramming*.

concurrent processing Synonymous with *multiprogramming*.

condensed pack A *pack* of cards in which, compared with an originating pack, the amount of data has been increased. A pack of cards for an *assembly program* may be input and used to produce a pack containing an equivalent *machine code* program. The output pack is known as the condensed pack, which is curious as it is, of course, the larger pack; but see also *condensing routine* which results in a condensed pack.
Also known as squoze pack.

condensing routine A *routine* for transferring an *object program* held in *memory* on to *punched cards* in such a way that the maximum number of *instructions* possible is contained on each card. ⟨⟩ *condensed pack*.

conditional branch instruction A *branch instruction* which transfers control to another *program* instruction only if a specified condition is satisfied; e.g. if a nominated item of data is one or more than one. If the specified condition is not satisfied the program carries on to the next instruction in the sequence.
Also known as conditional transfer or conditional jump.

conditional breakpoint A *breakpoint* at which the setting of certain conditions may allow variation in the particular *program* sequence.

conditional breakpoint instruction An *instruction* at a *breakpoint* which acts as a *conditional branch instruction* after the intervention resulting in the breakpoint has occurred.

conditional implication operation A *Boolean operation* in which the *result* for the values of the *operands* p and q is given by the table:

Operands		Result
p	q	r
0	0	1
1	0	0
0	1	1
1	1	1

Also known as If-Then operation, implication, inclusion, material implication.

conditional jump   Synonymous with *conditional branch instruction*.

conditional stop instruction   An *instruction* which causes a *program* to be stopped on the detection of a given condition such as the setting of a console switch by the operator.

conditional transfer   Synonymous with *conditional branch instruction*.

conditional transfer of control   To *transfer control* to another part of a *program* by means of a *conditional branch instruction*.

configuration   1. A general term given to a *computer system*. 2. The specific make-up of the physical units of a computer system, indicating the way in which the system is *configured*.

configuration state   The status of a device in a *configuration*[2], indicating its availability for use. ⬦ *configured-in, configured-off* and *configured-out*.

configure   To plan the appropriate component parts of a computer system to meet the requirements of a particular *application* or group of applications.

configured-in   The state of a device when its *configuration state* indicates that it is available for use. Related to *configured-out*, and contrasted with *configured-off*.

configured-off   The state of a device when its *configuration state* indicates that it is not available for use. Related to *configured-out* and contrasted with *configured-in*.

configured-out   The state of a device when its *configuration state* indicates that it is available for use only by certain privileged users. Related to *configured-in* and *configured-off*.

conjunction   Synonymous with *And operation*.

connective A symbol written between two *operands* and specifying the *operation* to be performed.

connector 1. A *flowchart* symbol, usually a small circle, used to indicate the connection between two different points on a flowchart. 2. A device used to terminate or connect electrical conductors.

console The computer unit used for communication between operators and system. The console usually includes a panel for display by means of lights and a typewriter, and allows further communication by keys and switches.

console display register A *register* which allows data (loaded by *program* or under operator control) to be displayed on the *console*.

console switch A *switch* which causes a *program* to alter its actions in accordance with the setting of the switch. The switch is set on the *console* by an operator.

console typewriter A unit of the *console* on which the computer can display messages to the operator and the operator can input *instructions* to the computer.

constant An item of data which does not vary in value; for example a numerical constant regularly required in a calculation.

constant area An area of *store* allocated by a *program,* used to hold *constants.*

construct A statement in a *source program* which will produce a particular effect when *executed.*

content The data held in a *storage* device or at a specific *location* in store.

content addressed storage Synonymous with *associative storage.*

contention 1. A rivalry for the use of a system resource. 2. Specifically the condition of a *communication channel* when two or more transmitting units are trying to transmit at the same time.

contrast In *optical character recognition,* the difference in colour, reflectance or shading of one area (e.g. a character) and the same characteristics of another area (e.g. the character's background).

control The function of selecting, interpreting and *executing instructions,* or carrying out required operations when certain specified conditions occur.

control card Synonymous with *parameter card.*

control character A character which initiates controlling operations over *peripheral units,* e.g. the control of carriage return on a *console typewriter.*
Also known as instruction character.

control circuits   The circuits in a *control unit* which carry out the *operations* initiated by *instructions*.

control counter   Synonymous with *control register*.

control language   ⋄ *job-control language*.

control loop   Synonymous with *control tape*.

control mark   Synonymous with *tape mark*.

control-message display   A device able to display control information (e.g. information on the operation of a *program* while it is being run) in plain language. The display might be, for example, on the *screen* of a *terminal* or on a typewriter.

control panel   1. A panel on a *console* containing keys and switches for manual communication with the *central processor*. 2. A special panel for the service engineer's controls.

control register   1. A *register* which contains the *address* of the next *instruction* in the sequence of operations. 2. The register which holds the address of the current instruction (more usually known as the instruction register).

Also known as carriage tape, control loop, paper tape loop.

control sequence   The usual order in which *instructions* are *executed*. A transfer of control is said to occur when a *branch instruction* changes the normal sequence.

control stack   A number of *storage locations* used to provide control in the *dynamic allocation* of work space.

control statement   Synonymous with *declarative statement*.

control tape   A *closed loop* of *paper tape* or plastic tape used to control the operation of some printing devices.

Also known as carriage tape, control loop, paper tape loop.

control total   A total established for a *file* or group of *records* during a specific operation such as a computer *run* to test whether the processing operation has been applied to all records. The total may be significant in itself, such as a total of all records in a specified value field, but may also be a *hash total*.

Also known as check total.

control transfer   The departure from a sequence of *instructions* which takes place when a *branch instruction* is obeyed.

control transfer instruction   Synonymous with *branch instruction*.

control unit   The circuits which carry out selection and retrieval of *instructions* from *storage* in sequence, interpret them and initiate the required *operation*.

control word   A *word* which specifies a particular action to be taken. The action depends on the type of control activity involved:

for example, the control word could supply the *parameters* directing an action, or it may specify *input/output* operations.

conventional A word which, like 'classical', in a computer context implies sound but old-fashioned. Conventional equipment once meant punched card tabulating equipment; it then meant machines with *core* storage and later came to mean centralized data processing in *batch* mode.

conversational Pertaining to *conversational mode*.

conversational compiler A *compiler* which uses *conversational mode*; the user enters each *source language* statement in turn to the computer, which immediately checks its validity (◊ *validity check*) and informs the user if he can continue or must correct a mistake. User and computer are thus engaged in dialogue.

conversational mode A method of operation in which the user at an *input/output terminal* is in direct communication with the computer and is able to obtain immediate response to his input messages, thus engaging in dialogue with the computer.
Also known as interactive mode.

conversion The process of changing the representation of data from one form to another, perhaps changing the *storage medium* or changing the code in which the data is held.
Also known as data conversion.

conversion program 1. A *program* designed to perform data *conversion*. 2. A program designed to convert programs written for one *computer system* into programs capable of being run on a different system. ◊ *simulator*.

convert To carry out the process of *conversion*.

copy To reproduce data from one *storage device* on another, or on another part of the same store, without altering the original data.

CORAL An acronym for Computer On-line Real-time Applications Language, a *high-level language* designed for *real time applications*.

core Throughout the 1960s it was common for *main memory* to be made up of small ferrite cores, each one capable of retaining a positive or negative charge and changing its charge when a current was passed through it. The memory was referred to as 'core store' and the term is still occasionally used inaccurately, if nostalgically, to refer to memory.

core store ◊ *core*.

corner cut A corner removed from a *punched card* so that all cards in a *pack* can be stacked the same way round before being fed to a machine.

corruption The mutilation of *code* or *data* caused by a *hardware* or *software* failure.

count 1. A cumulative total of the number of times a specific event occurs, kept as a factual record. 2. A total of the number of times a particular *instruction* is performed, kept for control purposes in, for example, *modification*.

counter A device used to accumulate totals and maintain a *count*.

counter, control Synonymous with *control register*.

CPM 1. Abbreviation for *critical path method*. 2. Abbreviation for cards per minute.

CPS 1. Abbreviation for characters per second. 2. Abbreviation for cycles per second.

CPU Abbreviation for central processing unit. ◊ *central processor*.

crash The result of a *hardware* or *software* malfunction; in particular a head crash when the *read/write head* of a *magnetic disk* unit touches the disk surface.

creation Initial *data collection* and subsequent organization into a *file*.

crippled leap-frog test A type of *leap-frog test* in which the test arithmetic is performed on only one part of *store*, rather than on different *locations*.

crippled mode A continuance of machine operation when the system is able to operate at reduced capacity in spite of the fact that certain parts are not working.

critical path method (CPM) A technique for defining jobs and events which must take place in order to accomplish specific objectives, and relating these jobs and events to each other on a time-scale. The interdependencies establish a network and the longest path through the network determines the duration of the project. This path is known as the critical path.
Also known as PERT, Program Evaluation and Review Technique.

cross check The checking of the result of a calculation by obtaining a solution to the problem by different methods and comparing the results.

cross compiler A *compiler* which produces *object code* in a format suitable for a different computer from the one on which the compiler is used.

cross talk The unwanted appearance of signals from one circuit on another circuit, causing interference.

CRT Abbreviation for *cathode ray tube*, often used as a synonym for *terminal* or video display unit.

cue An *instruction* containing a *key* for initiating entry to a *closed subroutine*.

cue-response query A query processed in such a way that it initiates a question–answer dialogue with the system. The response contains a cue leading to the next query.

current instruction register A *register* in which *instructions* are placed for execution under the control of the *program controller*.

cursor A *screen* character in a *terminal* display which indicates the location of the next character to be generated. The cursor can be moved to different positions of the screen by moving a *cursor key*.

cursor key A keyboard key used for manipulating the position on a *terminal screen* of a *cursor*.

cycle 1. A *loop* or sequence of operations carried out repetitively in the same order. 2. The time required for carrying out a given set of operations. 3. To repeat a set of operations a specified number of times.

cycle count A count of the number of times a cycle has been performed.

cycle index 1. The number of times a cycle of *instructions* has been completed. 2. The number of times a cycle of instructions remains to be completed in order to reach a specified number.

cycle reset Setting a *cycle index* or *cycle count* to its initial value or to some other specified value.

cycle stealing Synonymous with *direct memory access*.

cycle time The time taken to complete a *cycle*.

cyclic code Synonymous with *Gray code*.

cyclic shift A *shift* in which a *string* of *characters* or *bits* is treated as if it was a *closed loop*, so that data from one end of the string is re-entered at the other end.
Also known as circular shift.

cylinder In *magnetic disk* storage units, a set of corresponding *tracks* on a *stack* of disks.
Also known as seek area.

D

dagger operation   Synonymous with *Nor operation*.

daisy chain   Movement of signals from one unit to another in a serial fashion: daisy-chained *memory chips*, for example, are connected in such a way that *interrupt priorities* can be accepted by each chip, one after another.

daisy wheel   A serrated plastic disc around which is arranged a set of print *characters*. The wheel is rotated at speed until the desired character is brought before a hammer which strikes it against a ribbon. A daisy wheel can be easily exchanged for another with a different typeface.

damping   Reduction of amplitude and frequency of oscillation or wave motion.

data   Any group of *operands* or factors made up of numbers, alphabetic characters or symbols denoting any condition, value or state. Data is often distinguished from information (which is what is conveyed by data) and from *programs* (program *instructions* operate on data). The word data is commonly used as a collective noun attracting a singular verb and since the original singular 'datum' means 'a single piece of data' only in a very specialized sense, it is probably now wise to accept that English has embraced data as a singular noun, with a plural of 'data items' or 'groups of data'.

data access control   Any technique for transferring data between *main memory* and *input/output* devices.

data acquisition   Like *data collection*, but with the implication that data is collected *on-line*.

data adapter unit   A unit which allows a *central processor* to be connected to a number of data *communications channels*.

data administrator   1. A control element of a *data base management system*. 2. A person responsible for data definition and control in an organization using a data base management system.

data area   An area of *store* containing *data* rather than *instructions*.

data array   ◊ *array*.

data attribute   1. A characteristic of a *data* item, such as its value, length, or form. 2. A distinguishing feature of the entity represented by a data item, such as age, salary, colour of hair.

data bank A large *file* of *data* available to many users, usually by means of remote *terminals*. The implication of data bank is that widely diverse uses are made of the data and that to some extent it is available to the general public. Contrasted with *data base*[1].

data base 1. A *file* of *data* structured to allow a number of *applications* to access the data and update it without dictating or constraining the overall file design or content. 2. Any file which might sound more important if called a data base.

data base management system A complex *software* system designed to manage data in a *data base*[1], providing *security*, *dictionary* facilities and *resilience*.

data break Synonymous with *direct memory access*.

data bus ◊ *bus*.

data carrier Any medium such as paper, *punched cards*, *magnetic tape*, *magnetic disks*, for recording data.

data carrier store Any form of *data storage* in which the storage medium is external to the computer and data is held on a *data carrier*.

data cell Any *random-access storage device* which utilizes strips of *magnetic tape*.

data chaining Linking a *record* in one part of *memory* to another record by means of a *pointer*.

data channel multiplexor A *multiplexor* which services a number of *communications* channels, any of which may be transmitting or receiving data from a central computer. The communications channels may operate at varying speeds according to the needs of the system, but the multiplexor operates at a much higher speed to service these channels successively, one *character* at a time. ◊ *multiplexor*.

data collection The capturing of *raw data* either *on-line* at the instant a transaction occurs or *off-line* after the transaction has occurred. The term *data acquisition* is often given to the on-line process and data gathering to the more leisurely off-line process.

data communication 1. The transmission and reception of *data*. 2. The transmission, reception and validation of data, including interpretation, checking and verifying.

data compaction ◊ *compaction*.

data control The management of *data* entering or leaving a *data processing* system.

data conversion ◊ *conversion*.

data delimiter 1. Synonymous with *delimiter*. 2. A delimiter which not only *delimits* but also represents data in its own right.

data density Synonymous with *packing density*.

data description A statement in a *source program* that cannot be *executed* but describes the characteristics of the *data* to be operated on during the program.

data description language (DDL) A *language* used as part of a *data base management system* to describe the structure and relationships of *data elements*, *records* and *files*.

data dictionary Synonymous with *dictionary*.

data display unit Synonymous with *terminal*.

data element A set of *data items* which can be considered in a given situation as a unit.

data element chain An ordered set of two or more *data elements* used as a single data element.
Also known as macroelement.

data format The way *data* is held in a *file*, e.g. in *character* form.

data gathering ◊ *data collection*.

data item One of the units of data contained in a *record* describing a particular *data attribute*. Part of a *data element*.

data level The hierarchical position of a particular *data element* in relation to other elements specified as part of the same *record* in a *source language*.

data link The equipment used in connecting one location with another for the purpose of transmitting and receiving data.
Also known as communication link.

data logger A device capable of capturing information and recording it as it occurs – for example, recording minute-by-minute changes in air pollution or room temperature.

data management 1. The control and direction of *data collection*, analysis, indexing, *storage*, *retrieval* and distribution. 2. The *software* used to provide *data manipulation*. ⊅ *data base management system*.

data manipulation The process undertaken in a *data base management system* of defining operations required by users in processing data and then carrying out the operations.

data matrix An *array* of values stored in rows and columns which represent *variables* and the values they may take.

data name A descriptive label allocated by a programmer to a *record* or *field*. ⊅ *dictionary*.

data network An arrangement of *data terminal* equipment, *data communication* equipment and *data links*.

data phone A device which allows *data* to be transferred over a telephone line.

data plotter A device which provides a visual display, usually in the form of a graph on paper, by plotting the course of coordinates calculated in the *central processor* to which the data plotter is linked. Also known as x-y plotter.

data preparation The process of converting to machine-readable form *data* which has been gathered *off-line*.

data processing The operations performed on *data* in order to derive *information* or to achieve order among *files* for later access.

data purification The process of *validating* and correcting data to reduce the number of errors entering a *data processing* system.

data record A *record* containing a unit of data for processing by a *program*.

data reduction The process of deriving useful, organized data from a mass of *raw data*. The process may be carried out before computer input or the reduction may itself be carried out by computer, sometimes *on-line* to the source of data.

data representation The use of *characters* to represent values and descriptive data.

data set 1. An electronic device which provides an *interface* between a *data processing* machine and a telephone or telegraph communication line. 2. A combination of *data* elements, not all of which need to be present at one time. For example, payroll information for each employee may form a data set, but not all employees will be subject to all deductions.

data sink Equipment in a *data communications* system which accepts data signals from a transmission device. Contrasted with *data source*.

data source Equipment in a *data communications* system which originates data signals for a transmission device. Contrasted with *data sink*.

data station A unit incorporating *input/output* equipment and which is connected to a telephone or telegraph circuit by a *data set*[1] to allow direct communication with a central computer.

data storage The use of any medium for storing data, with the implication of the ability to store large volumes of data *on-line* to a *central processor*.

data-switching centre An installation in a *data communications* system in which data in the form of messages is routed in accordance with instructions contained in the message itself or in accordance with *program instructions*. Switching equipment is used to interconnect communication circuits.

data terminal   A remote station which is capable of modulating, encoding, demodulating and decoding data between an *input/output* device and a *data transmission* line.

data transmission   The automatic transfer of data from one computer system to another, or to and from a central computer and remote *data collection* points.

data unit   A group of one or more *characters* related so that they form a whole. Similar to (but not always synonymous with) *field*[1], and related to *data set*[2].

data word   A unit of *data* stored in a single *word* of a *storage* medium.

DC   Abbreviation for direct current or direct coupled.

DC amplifier   ⟡ *direct-coupled amplifier*.

DDE   Abbreviation for *direct data entry*.

DDL   Abbreviation for *data description language*.

dead band   Synonymous with *dead zone*.

dead halt   ⟡ *drop-dead halt*.

deadlock   Synonymous with *deadly embrace*.

deadly embrace   When all processes within a computer are competing for resources at the same time, and all are suspended at the same time. Until external intervention removes one process and allows the others to be reactivated, no one process can continue and all action is frozen.
Also known as deadlock.

dead time   A delay deliberately introduced between two activities in order to avoid interference between them.

dead zone   A range of input values for a signal which can be changed but have no effect on the output signal.
Also known as dead band.

dead zone unit   A device used on an *analog computer*, to give a constant output signal over a predetermined range of an input variable.

deallocate   To restore the availability of a system resource.

deblocking   The process of extracting *records* from a *block* of data so that the individual records can be processed.

debugging   The process of testing a *program* and removing faults. Ideally, a single phase in the development of a program in which the program is run with test data to test all *branches* and conditions that may exist in the program. Unhappily, debugging can often continue throughout the working life of a program.

debugging aid routine Any routine used by programmers when testing *programs*. For example, a *diagnostic routine* or a routine for producing a *memory dump*.

Also known as checkout routine.

decade A group of ten items. For example, a group of ten *storage locations*.

decay time The time required for an ephemeral phenomenon to reach a particular fraction of its original value; e.g. the time taken for a voltage to decrease to one tenth of its original value.

deceleration time The time required to stop moving, from the moment at which the stopping action is initiated to the moment of stopping. For example, the time required for a moving *magnetic tape* to come to a halt, measured from the completion of a *read* or *write* operation to the time when the tape has stopped moving.

Also known as stop time.

decentralized data processing The processing of data by each sub-unit in an organization. Contrasted with centralized *data processing* where a central computing installation receives data from sub-units, processes it and returns results.

decibel One tenth of a bel: a unit of power level, measuring signal loss or gain in a transmission circuit. The unit is often used to express a level of intensity of sound.

decimal notation The system of writing numbers in which successive digit positions are represented by successive powers of the *radix* ten. Decimal numbers are often represented in computers by *binary digits* arranged in groups of four, each group corresponding to a single digit of a decimal number. ⟡ *binary coded decimal notation*.

decimal notation, coded ⟡ *binary coded decimal notation*.

decimal numeral A number represented in *decimal notation*; i.e. one using the decimal digits from the range 0, 1, 2, 3, 4, 5, 6, 7, 8, and 9.

decimal point The *radix* point in the *decimal notation* system used to denote the separation of the integral and fractional parts of a *decimal numeral*.

decision A choice made between two or more possible courses; an operation performed by a computer to choose between such courses of action, usually made by comparing the relative magnitude of two specified *operands*. A *branch instruction* is then used to select the required path.

decision box A *flowchart* symbol used to represent a *decision* or *branch* in a sequence of *program instructions*.

decision element Synonymous with *threshold element*.

decision instruction An *instruction* which discriminates between the relative values of two specified *operands*.

decision table A method of presenting the relationship between certain *variables* in order to specify the required action when various conditions are present. These tables may be used to assist in developing solutions to problems, and are often used instead of *flowcharts* or in conjunction with flowcharts to display relationships between items in a system or *program*. Some *programming languages* have been written to make direct use of decision tables when a problem is specified.

deck 1. Synonymous with *pack*[1]. 2. Synonymous with *tape deck*.

deck, tape ◇ *tape deck*.

declaration Synonymous with *declarative statement*.

declarative Synonymous with *declarative statement*.

declarative macro A *statement* which instructs a *compiler* or *assembler* to carry out some action or to react to some condition. A declarative macro does not result in an action to be taken by the *object program*.

declarative statement A *statement* in a *source program* which specifies to the *compiler* the format, size and nature of data elements and constants used as *operands* in the program.
Also known as control statement, declarative, declarative macro, directive.

decoder A device used to alter data from one coded format to another. The device is usually a network in which a combination of input signals produces an output signal on one or more of a number of output lines.

decrement 1. The amount by which the magnitude of a *variable* is reduced. 2. To reduce the magnitude of a variable. ◇ *decrement field*.

decrement field The part of an *instruction word* used for *modifying* the contents of a *storage location* or *register*.

decryption The decoding of *coded*[3] *data*.

dedicated A *program*, procedure, *line*[1], machine or system set apart for special use.

default Synonymous with *default option*.

default option An option or value that is to be assumed if no other has been specified.

Also known as default.

deferred addressing   A method of *indirect addressing* in which an indirect address is replaced by another address. This procedure occurs a specified number of times or until it is ended by the setting of an *indicator*.

degauss   To demagnetize a *magnetic tape* by use of a *degausser*.

degausser   A coil momentarily energized by an alternating current, with the function of rearranging the signals on a *magnetic tape*.

degeneracy   The state occasioned by *negative feedback*.

degradation   A reduction of system capability while still maintaining a level of service. ⟡ *graceful degradation*.

delay counter   A counter used to insert a deliberate time delay so that an operation external to the *program* may take place.

delay element   An element which delays a signal by introducing a time delay.

delay element, digit   ⟡ *digit delay element*.

delay line   A device with one input channel and a number of output channels in which signals are deliberately delayed, introducing a time lag into the process of transmitting data; usually in order to ensure the arrival of data from several points at one point at the same time.

delay line, acoustic   ⟡ *acoustic delay line*.

delay line, Hg   Synonymous with *mercury delay line*.

delay line register   A *storage register* in which data is stored in serial representation by the continual recirculation of a signal. The register incorporates a *delay line*, a means for signal regeneration and a feedback channel.

delay line, sonic   Synonymous with *acoustic delay line*.

delay line store   A *dynamic store* which uses a *delay line* whose output is *amplified* and re-input, causing the pulses to circulate indefinitely. In this way data circulates in the store without alteration until it is no longer required, when the loop is interrupted.

delete   1. An operation to remove or eliminate an item, *record* or group of records from a *file*. 2. To erase a *program* from *memory*, e.g. at the end of a *run*.

deletion record   A *change record* which causes the deletion of one or more existing records on a master *file*.

delimit   To establish the bounds of a group of related *characters*, by the use of special marker characters known as *delimiters*, not in themselves members of the group. (But ⟡ *data delimiter*.)

delimiter A marker *character* used to *delimit* the bounds of a group of characters.

demand processing In demand processing mode, data is accepted from an external device immediately and processed at once, subject only to system priorities. It is thus unnecessary to store *raw data* for later *batch processing*.
Also known as immediate processing, in-line processing.

demodulation The process of reconstituting an original signal from a *modulated* signal; the reverse of the *modulation* process.

demodulator A device capable of performing the *demodulation* function; in *data transmission*, for example, it receives audio tones and converts them to electrical pulses.

denial, alternative Synonymous with *Not-And operation*.

denial, joint Synonymous with *Nor operation*.

dense list A list of the contents of certain contiguous *storage areas*. Also known as linear list.

dependent program A *program* called in by an *operating system* when required; e.g. a *user program* or a *utility program*.

deposit Synonymous with *dump*[1].

deque A double-ended *queue*, allowing deletions or insertions at either end.

description list A list of *data elements* and their attributes.

descriptor A significant element of data used in, and descriptive of, a *record*, allowing the record to be classified, sorted and retrieved.

designator That part which classifies; e.g. in a number the least significant digit classifies whether the number is odd or even.

desk check Synonymous with *dry run*.

despatch To allocate the time of a *central processor* to a specific job which the *despatcher* has placed in an execution state.

despatcher The process in an *operating system* which carries out the switching functions to result in the correct sources and destinations of *words* being transferred.

destructive addition Addition after which the *sum* appears in the *location* previously occupied by an *operand*, usually the *augend*. The operand is thus destroyed.

destructive read A *read* operation in which data is taken from a *location* to another destination in such a way that the data in the original location is lost or mutilated. ⊘ *destructive storage*.

destructive storage A *storage device* in which *read* operations are destructive and the contents of which must therefore be regenerated after being read if they are required at the same *location* after a read operation. ⟨⟩ *destructive read.*

detail file   Synonymous with *change file.*

detected error   An error which is discovered before output from a system is produced. The implication is that the error is noted but not corrected.

de-update   A *recovery* procedure in which an earlier version of a *file* is re-created by replacement of those *records* which have recently been updated by versions of the records taken from copies of the file made at an earlier processing stage.

device control character   A *control character* used in *data communications* systems; its function when transmitted is to cause a device to be switched on or off.

device flag   A *register* consisting of one *bit* with the function of recording the status of a *peripheral unit.* ⟨⟩ *device status word.*

device queue   A queue of requests to use a device.

device status word   A *word* in which the condition of the *bits* indicates the status of *peripheral units.* ⟨⟩ *device flag.*

diad   Synonymous with *doublet.*

diagnosis   The process of locating and explaining errors in *software*, or failures in *hardware.*

diagnostic check   Synonymous with *diagnostic test.*

diagnostic program   Synonymous with *diagnostic routine.*

diagnostic routine   A general-purpose *routine* used to trace coding errors in a *program*, or operator error, or a machine malfunction. Also known as diagnostic program.

diagnostic test   A test designed to locate malfunctions or potential malfunctions, usually by the use of a *diagnostic routine.* Also known as diagnostic check.

dial-up   The ability to use a dial telephone to initiate a line connection between a remote *terminal* and a central computer, thus avoiding the need for the terminal to be *on-line* at all times.

dichotomizing search   Synonymous with *binary chop.*

dictionary   A table specifying the size and format of *operands* in a *file*, identifying each *record* and *field* type by a *data name.* Dictionaries have varying degrees of complexity and when used in connection with *data base management systems* fulfil many functions related to specification of size and structure of files. Also known as data dictionary.

difference   The result obtained by subtracting one number from another.

difference, symmetric Synonymous with *Exclusive-Or* operation.

differential amplifier A circuit which produces an output signal derived from the difference between two input signals.

differentiator A device whose output is proportional to the differential of the input with respect to one or more *variables*.

diffusion In *semiconductor* production, the process of introducing minute quantities of impurity into a *substrate* material such as silicon, allowing the impurity to spread into the substrate.

digit A *character* which represents an integer smaller than the *radix* of the relevant number system; a character position in a number which may assume any such value. For example, the number 6673 consists of four digits but only three types of character.

digital Pertaining to the use of discrete signals to represent data in the form of numbers or *characters* to any required degree of *precision*. Contrasted with *analog*, where data is continuous but the degree of precision is limited by the capability of the devices used to express the data.

digital adder ⋄ *adder*.

digital/analog converter A device able to convert *digital* signals into a continuous signal suitable for input to an *analog computer*.

digital computer A computer which operates on *variables* expressed as data in discrete form. Data and *program instructions* are recorded as *code*[2] *characters*, and the term digital computer is usually taken to imply a *stored program* which may modify its own action.

digital incremental plotter An output device which accepts *digital* signals from a *central processor* and uses them to activate a plotting pen and a paper-carrying drum.

digital read-out An immediate display of data in digital form, e.g. using light-emitting *diodes* or liquid crystal. Wrist-watches display data either in analog form (hands) or as digital read-out (digits).

digital representation The representation of *variables* by means of discrete quantities or *digits*.

digital resolution The value given to the least significant *digit* of a number.

digit compression Any technique for increasing the number of *digits* which may be *stored* in a specific storage area, and thus reducing the physical size of a *file*. Data may be *packed*[2] for storage and later *unpacked* for processing.

digit delay element A logic device for introducing a *delay element* of one digit period.

digitize   To express data in *digital* form; e.g. to convert an *analog* representation such as a voltage to a digital form of representation.

digitizer   A device which can convert an *analog* measurement to a *digital* form.

digit period   The time interval for each single digital signal in a series, determined by the *pulse repetition frequency* of the computer.
Also known as digit time.

digit place   Synonymous with *digit position*.

digit position   In *positional notation*, the site of each digit in a number, usually identified by a number starting with the lowest significant digit.
Also known as digit place.

digits, equivalent binary   ◊ *equivalent binary digits*.

digit time   Synonymous with *digit period*.

diminished radix complement   A number derived by the subtraction of each digit of a specified number from one less than the equivalent *radix*. ◊ *complement*.

diode   A device with two terminals which allows current to flow in one direction only, and thus acts as a switching device to control current flow in an associated circuit. Originally used to describe a thermionic valve with only two plates (cathode and anode); nowadays diodes are formed by a junction of a base metal and a crystalline element such as germanium or silicon.

DIP   Abrreviation for *dual in-line package*.

direct access   Synonymous with *random access*.

direct address   Synonymous with *absolute address*.

direct allocation   Allocation of specific *peripheral units* and *storage locations* at the time of programming. Contrasted with *dynamic allocation*.

direct code   Synonymous with *absolute code*.

direct coding   *Instructions* written in *absolute code.*

direct-coupled amplifier   An *amplifier* which amplifies input signals regardless of how slowly such signals vary. The amplifier uses resistors for coupling signals in and out of the active element.
Also known as DC amplifier, direct-current amplifier, directly coupled amplifier.

direct-coupled flip-flop   A *flip-flop* constructed of electronic circuits in which the active elements are coupled with transistors.

direct-current amplifier   Synonymous with *direct-coupled amplifier*.

direct data entry   (DDE) *Input* of data direct to a computer without a previous *off-line data preparation* process.

direct-insert routine   Synonymous with *open routine*.

direct-insert subroutine   ◊ *open routine*.

direct instruction   An *instruction* which directly addresses the *operand* on which a specified *operation* is to be performed.

directive   Synonymous with *declarative statement*.

directly coupled amplifier   Synonymous with *direct-coupled amplifier*.

direct memory access   (DMA) High-speed data transfer direct between an *input/output* channel and *memory*.
Also known as cycle stealing, data break.

director   A control *program*, usually part of an *operating system* and controlling the allocation of resources within the system.

directory   1. Synonymous with *dictionary*. 2. Sometimes given the special meaning of a system of organizing *software* into *files*.

direct serial file organization   Organization of *files* on a *random access* device, allowing individual *records* to be accessed and updated directly on the device without affecting other records.

disable   To inhibit or remove some *hardware* or *software* feature; e.g. to suppress an *interrupt* facility.

disarm   To disallow an *interrupt*. Contrasted with *arm*.

disaster dump   A *dump* occurring as a result of a non-recoverable machine or *program* error.

disc   ◊ *magnetic disk*.

discrete   Pertaining to data organized in separate distinct parts, such as an electrical pulse or a graphic character.

discrimination instruction   Synonymous with *branch instruction*.

disjunction   Synonymous with *Or operation*.

disjunctive search   A search to retrieve *records* containing at least one of a given set of keys; relating to *Or operations*. (Disjunction is synonymous with Or.)

disk   ◊ *magnetic disk*.

disk drive   The transport mechanism of a *magnetic disk* unit, causing the movement of the magnetic medium.

diskette   Synonymous with *floppy disk*.

disk file   ◊ *magnetic disk file*.

disk file controller   A device which controls the transfer of data between a number of *magnetic disk* units and *main memory*.

disk pack   A removable assembly of *magnetic disks* capable of being easily placed on and removed from a *disk drive* unit.

dispatch   ◊ *despatch*.

disperse   To distribute *items* from an *input record* to several locations in one or more *output records*. Input items are thus dispersed among more *data sets*[1] than they originally occupied.

dispersed intelligence   Synonymous with *distributed intelligence*.

dispersion   Synonymous with *Not-And operation*.

display   An operation which results in a visual record; in particular one in which a message or selected data is output to an operator for visual inspection. Data may be output as a printed report, but the implication is that it appears in graphic or character form on a *terminal screen*.

display console   A unit used to interrogate *files* or *memory* areas in order to display *data* currently being processed or already *stored*.

display console, message   ◊ *message display console*.

display control   An *interface* unit used to connect a number of *terminals* to a *central processor*.

display menu   The options listed by a *display* for selection by the operator, who selects the next action by means of an input device such as a *keypad*, *keyboard* or *light pen*.

display tube   ◊ *cathode ray tube* and *terminal*.

distance   Synonymous with *Exclusive-Or* operation. ◊ *signal distance*.

distributed intelligence   1. In a *decentralized data processing* system *applications programs* and *system control* functions are carried out to a greater or lesser degree by the distributed remote units, according to the degree of *intelligence* or processing capability owned by these units. ◊ *dumb terminals*, *smart terminals*, *intelligent terminals*, and *front-end processors*. 2. A distributed intelligence system is one in which multiple microprocessors each carry out a fixed function. Contrasted with *multiprocessing*, where tasks are allocated according to load.
Also known as dispersed intelligence.

diversity   Synonymous with *Exclusive-Or* operation.

dividend   An *operand* used in *division*. The dividend is divided by the *divisor* to produce the *quotient* and *remainder*.

divider   A device which performs the arithmetic function of *division*, and obtains as an output the quotient of two input variables, the *dividend* and the *divisor*.

division   An arithmetic operation in which one *operand*, the *dividend*, is divided by another, the *divisor*, to produce the *quotient* and *remainder*.

division subroutine   A *subroutine* which carries out the arithmetic operation of *division*. Usually achieved by an *algorithm* which selects trial digits for the *quotient* and repeatedly subtracts the *divisor* from the *dividend* until the *difference* is negative – at which point the subroutine recognizes that the trial quotient was too large.

divisor An *operand* used in *division*. The *divisor* is divided into the *dividend* to produce the *quotient* and *remainder*.

DMA Abbreviation for *direct memory access*.

DMOS Abbreviation for double-diffused metal oxide *semiconductor*.

document 1. Any form or voucher containing details of some *transaction*. The implication is that a 'document is made of paper rather than a magnetic medium and that it has some degree of permanency. 2. To document is to carry out the process of *documentation*.

documentation The process of collecting, organizing and presenting information relating to a computer system; documentation is necessary to provide a source of reference for all manual and automatic procedures forming part of that system. For example, a *systems definition* must be documented to include *source document* specifications, *file layouts*, flowcharts of procedures, *print formats*, *card formats*, and *narrative* to explain the objectives and operations of the system. *Programming* documentation includes all *block flowcharts*, *micro flowcharts*, *coding sheets*, *data formats*, and narrative to describe detailed programming procedures. *Operating instructions* also form an important part of the documentation for a system. Standard techniques are usually adopted within a particular data processing organization to ensure that an orderly record is made at every step in the development of a system.

documentation book A collection of all the *documentation* relevant to a particular *program* or system.

document, original ◊ *source document*.

docuterm A word or phrase used to describe the contents of a *document* and which may be used in subsequent *retrieval* as a *data name*.

donor An element which is introduced in minute quantities as an impurity to a semiconducting material. The donor has a negative valence greater than the valence of the semiconductor in its pure form.

do-nothing instruction An *instruction* which performs no action during the operation of a *program*. It has no functional significance, but may, for example, allow for future changes to the program or to complete a group of instructions where the *machine* *code* system requires instructions to be written in complete *blocks*. Also known as blank instruction, dummy instruction, no-operation instruction, null instruction, waste instruction.

dopant A chemical impurity added to a semiconductor material to change its electrical characteristics.

doped Subjected to *dopant*.

dot matrix printer A *printer* in which each character is made up of a matrix of dots formed by wires, styluses, or jets.

double-ended queue ⟡ *deque*.

double-length number Synonymous with *double-precision number*.

double-precision arithmetic Relating to arithmetic operations performed with *operands* which each occupy two *words*, allowing greater *precision* to be obtained in the result.

double-precision number A number stored in two *words* in *memory* for use in *double-precision arithmetic*.
Also known as double-length number.

doublet A *byte* consisting of two *binary* elements.
Also known as diad.

down time The period during which a machine is not operating because of a machine fault.

DPM 1. Abbreviation for data processing manager. 2. Abbreviation for documents per minute.

drift A change in the output of a circuit (e.g. a *direct-coupled amplifier*) which takes place very slowly. The change is usually caused by a voltage fluctuation or some change in the circuit's environment.

drift-corrected amplifier A type of amplifier used in an *analog computer*; includes circuits designed to reduce *drift*.

drift error In *analog computers*, an error caused by *drift*.

drive 1. Any device which causes the movement of a recording medium, such as a *disk drive* or *tape deck*; also known as a tape drive. 2. Any circuit which generates a pulse to operate an electro-mechanical device.

drive, magnetic tape ⟡ *tape deck*.

driver A *program* that controls a *peripheral unit* connected *on-line*.

DRO Abbreviation for destructive read out. ⟡ *destructive read*.

drop-dead halt A machine halt from which there is no recovery. The halt may be deliberately *programmed* to take place if a specified condition occurs or it may be the result of a logical error in programming (e.g. division by zero).
Also known as a dead halt.

drop-in The accidental generation of spurious *bits* during reading from or writing to a *magnetic memory* medium. Contrasted with *drop-out*.

drop-out The accidental failure to read or write a *character*, *digit* or *bit* to a *magnetic memory*. The failure is usually caused by a flaw such as dirt or a scratch or other blemish on the magnetic surface.

drum ◊ *magnetic drum*.

dry run The process of examining the logic and *coding* of a *program*, checking the *flowcharts* and written *instructions*, checking the result of each step before the program is actually run on a computer.

Also known as desk check.

dual in-line package (DIP) Integrated circuits enclosed in a package which takes its name from the double parallel rows of pins connecting to the *circuit board*.

dual operation A *Boolean operation* which has the result of negating the result of another Boolean operation that is applied to the negation of the *operands*. The *truth table* of a dual operation can be obtained by reversing the value of each element in the table of another operation.

dual port memory A *memory* unit with dual data and *address* connections, suitable for low-level (◊ *low-level language*) communication between microprocessors.

dual processor system A configuration which includes two *central processors*, each receiving the same *input* and *executing* the same *routines*. The results of each process may be compared. Such duplication is cost-effective when very high reliability is required.

Also known as dual system.

dual system ◊ *dual processor system*.

dumb terminal A *terminal* device which can receive and/or transmit signals and therefore act as an *input* and/or *output* device, but which has no local processing capability. The dumbness refers to lack of intelligence rather than any inability to produce voice output. ◊ *smart terminal*, *intelligent terminal*.

dummy An artificial item (such as an *address*, *instruction* or *routine*) inserted in order to satisfy a logical or structural requirement but which does not itself directly affect a machine operation except to allow other operations to be carried out. ◊ *do-nothing instruction*.

dummy instruction Synonymous with *do-nothing instruction*.

dump 1. To copy the contents of an area of *memory* to a *backing* *store*. The process of dumping may be carried out regularly during the running of a *program*, especially during long runs involving slow *input/output peripheral units*, to ensure that if the job is interrupted then the program can be restarted from the last *dump point* without the need to start again from the beginning of the run. 2. The accidental or intentional withdrawal of power from a computer.

dump and restart The techniques involved in ensuring that a *run* can be satisfactorily restarted after a *dump*[2]. These include the *programming* techniques of arranging *dump points* and *dump checks*, and *operating* techniques of recording dump points, preserving dump information and re-setting *peripheral units*.

dump check A check carried out to ensure that a *dump*[1] has been correctly made or correctly re-started; for example, by totalling all values in a certain field on a transfer to *backing store* and verifying that sum when the data is transferred back to *memory*.

dump point That step in a *program* at which a *dump*[1] is initiated.

duodecimal number system A number system in which each digit position has a *radix* of twelve.

duplex A method of communication between two terminals in which each can transmit to the other simultaneously. ⊘ *half-duplex* and *simplex*.

Also known as full duplex.

duplex channel A *channel* allowing simultaneous transmission in both directions. ⊘ *duplex*.

duplex computer An *on-line* configuration in which two identical computer systems are employed, one acting as a standby to safeguard against the failure or shutdown for maintenance of the other.

duplicated record An exact copy of a *record*, perhaps retained on a different medium, kept to safeguard against loss or mutilation of the original record. But ⊘ *duplicate record*.

duplicate record An unwanted *record* in a *file*, with the same *key* as another record in the same file. But ⊘ *duplicated record*.

duplication check An operation which involves the comparison of the results of two calculations; each calculation attempts to solve the same problem, but each uses a different method. Related to *arithmetic check*.

dwell A programmed time delay of variable duration.

dyadic Boolean operation An operation in which a *Boolean algebra* process is specified and where the result is determined by the *bit* patterns of each of two *operands* and the *truth table* of the *operator*[2].

Also known as binary Boolean operation.

dyadic operation   An *operation*[1] using two *operands*.

Also known as binary operation.

dynamic allocation   One of the tasks of an *operating system* in a *multiprogramming* environment, involving the provision of such resources as *storage* areas, *peripheral units* and *programs* on demand rather than as a result of prior scheduling.

dynamic buffering   A technique of operating a *buffer* so that when a *program* is in need of a buffer one is provided in response to a demand. In the same way, the *storage* area allocated as a buffer is extended or contracted by the addition or removal of storage units while the messages for which the buffer is needed are arriving.

dynamic dump   A *dump* carried out during the execution of a *program*.

dynamicizer   A *logical element* which converts a set of *digits* represented by the spatial distribution of *bits* in *store* into a sequence of signals distributed in time.

dynamic memory   Synonymous with *dynamic store*.

dynamic RAM   ⬦ *dynamic store*.

dynamic stop   The use of a *branch instruction* to create a *program loop* which is in turn used to draw attention to an *error* condition.

dynamic storage allocation   In a *multiprogramming* environment (when a number of *programs* are likely to be operating in *memory* at the same time) the most efficient utilization of storage; this is made by allocating storage in such a way that storage areas assigned to programs and data are assigned according to their precise need in accordance with program priorities.

dynamic store   1. A regenerative *store* in which data is retained as a result of the continual circulation of a signal (e.g. transmitting data in a *delay line*) or by moving the medium. 2. A store in which dynamic circuits use the presence or absence of a charge on a capacitor. Since the capacitor has a leakage current the stored data degrades slowly and must be refreshed periodically.

Also known as circulating storage, dynamic memory, dynamic RAM.

dynamic subroutine   A *subroutine* which, each time it is entered, requires *parameters* to specify the particular action to be performed.

E

EAM Abbreviation for electrical accounting machines, *punched card* and punched *paper tape data processing* equipment, predominantly electromechanical as opposed to electronic.

EAROM Acronym for electrically alterable *read-only memory*.

earth station A *terminal* able to transmit, receive and process data communicated via a satellite.

EBCDIC Abbreviation for Extended Binary Coded Decimal Interchange Code, a widely recognized code with a *character set* of 8-*bit* coded characters.

EBR Abbreviation for *electron beam recording*.

Eccles Jordan circuit Synonymous with *flip-flop*.

echo Part of a transmitted signal reflected back with enough magnitude and delay to be recognizable and thus received as interference.

echo check A *check* on the accuracy of *data transmission*; data already transmitted is returned to the point from which it was sent and compared with the original data.

ECL Abbreviation for *emitter coupled logic*.

edge card A *circuit board* which has contact strips along one of its edges. This edge fits into a *mother board* and the contact strips mate with *edge connectors*.

edge connector An electrical socket on a *mother board* into which a contact strip on an *edge card* can slot.

edit To prepare data for subsequent processing. The process of editing may involve validation, deletion of data not required, conversion of fields to *internal format* (e.g. value *fields*[1] to be converted to *binary*), *code conversion*, and preparation of data for subsequent output, e.g. *zero suppression*.

editor 1. A *routine* whose function is to carry out *editing* operations (a) on input data and *programs* before or during a computer *run* or (b) on output data at the end of the run. Also known as edit routine. 2. *Software* which allows the *interactive* review and editing of a program or data.

edit routine Synonymous with *editor*[1].

EDP Abbreviation for *electronic data processing*.

EDS Abbreviation for *exchangeable disk store*.

EEROM Acronym for electrically erasable *read-only memory* – a ROM unit which need not be removed from its socket to be erased.

effective In microprocessor cant, the word effective tends to mean 'actual'. Contrasted with *virtual*.

effective address An *address* used by the computer in *executing* an *instruction*, as opposed to the address originally written in the *program*. The difference normally results from *instruction modification*.

effective data-transfer rate The rate of data transmission, not including *peripheral unit* starting, stopping, searching or other peripheral unit operations subject to *program* control.
Also known as effective transmission rate.

effective instruction Synonymous with *actual instruction*.

effective transmission rate Synonymous with *effective data-transfer rate*.

eight-bit-byte Synonymous with *octet*.

Either-Or operation Synonymous with *Or operation*.

either-way operation Synonymous with *half-duplex*.

elapsed time The total time apparently required to complete an activity, measured from the start to the finish. This time may be longer than the actual activity time, since periods of inactivity, while other processes are taking place, may be included in the elapsed time measurement.

electrical tough pitch A grade of copper, known as ETP, used in electrical conductors.

electron beam recording (EBR) A beam of electrons directed on to an energy-sensitive film is used to produce microfilm containing computer-generated data. Electron beam recording techniques are also used to produce *random access* devices.

electronic data processing (EDP) Data processing performed by electronic machines; the methods and techniques associated with such processing.

electronic differential analyser An incremental computer which uses *digital* representations for the *analog* quantities in an analog differential analyser.

electrostatic storage A *storage device* which represents data in the form of the presence or absence of an electrostatic charge on a non-conducting surface such as the screen of a *cathode ray tube*.
Also known as cathode ray tube storage.

else rule A logical rule which covers conditions not covered by other explicit rules: the rule defines the operations to be performed if none of the explicitly described conditions occurs.

EM character Abbreviation for *end-of-medium character*.

emitter coupled logic (ECL) A method of connecting circuits to meet high speed requirements; extra *diffusions* are needed in the manufacturing process thus increasing the cost of emitter coupled logic *memory*.

empty medium A medium which contains no useful data, but has been prepared to accept such data by having some preliminary data recorded in it, e.g. *magnetic tape* with *header labels* already written. Contrasted with *virgin medium*. ⌀ *data carrier*.

empty string Synonymous with *null string*.

emulate To use a computer to operate on data and *instructions* prepared for a computer of a different type, perhaps requiring special *software* and *hardware* to represent the original computer's facilities. ⌀ *emulator*.

emulator A *hardware* (and sometimes *software*) device built into a computer of one type but used to run jobs originally written for a computer of another type. The emulator thus accepts existing *programs* and data without requiring them to be rewritten for the new computer.

emulator generation The process of assembling and linking an *emulator* during *sysgen*.

enable To restore to ordinary operating conditions; e.g. to remove an inhibiting signal, or to restore a suppressed feature. ⌀ *enabling signal*.

enabling signal A *signal* which allows a previously set up operation to take place.

encode To apply the rules of a code, representing data in digital form denoting *characters* or symbols.

encoder A circuit which converts, for example, the single switch closures resulting from key depressions on a keyboard to a composite code suitable for a further processing stage.

end-around carry A *carry* generated in the *most significant character* position, causing a carry into the *least significant character* position.

end-around shift Synonymous with *logical shift*.

end mark A *code* used to signal the end of a unit of data.

end of data A code which indicates the end of all data held on a particular *storage* unit (e.g. a reel of magnetic tape). This is not necessarily the end of the *file*; ◊ *end-of-file marker*.

end-of-file indicator   Synonymous with *end-of-file marker*.

end-of-file marker   A marker which indicates (to *hardware* and *software*) the end of a *file*, i.e. the fact that no more data can be written to the file.

Also known as end-of-file indicator, end-of-file spot.

end-of-file spot   Synonymous with *end-of-file marker*.

end-of-medium character   A control character indicating the physical limit of a data medium.

Also known as EM character.

end-of-message character   A character used to indicate the end of a message.

end-of-record word   A *word* which terminates a *record*, usually in a specific format, allowing the end of the record to be identified.

end-of-transmission character   (EOT) A transmission control character used to indicate the completion of a transmission.

ENQ   Abbreviation for enquiry character. ◊ *inquiry character*.

enquiry   ◊ *inquiry*.

entry   1. The *address* of the first *instruction* in a *program* to be obeyed. 2. The first instruction of a *subroutine*. 3. Any unit of information, either input or output; an item of data in a *list*[2] or *table*.

entry block   That part of *store* into which an *entry*[3] or unit of data is placed on input.

entry condition   A specified condition which must be met before a *routine* is entered.

Also known as initial condition.

entry instruction   The *instruction* obeyed on *entry*[1] to a *routine*. Some routines may have a number of *entry points* and the entry instruction will depend on *entry conditions* at the time of entry.

entry point   The first *instruction* to be obeyed in a *routine*. A routine may have several entry points, each one relating to different *entry conditions*.

envelope   To arrange, by the provision for example of special *labels*, for a *file* established on one type of computer to be catalogued and handled on another type of computer.

environment   1. The physical conditions surrounding a computer installation including heat, pressure, pollution, vibration. 2. The elements (physical, organizational, personal, political) which influence the design and operation of a system. 3. The mode of operation of a computer, e.g. a *multiprogramming* environment.

EOF Abbreviation for end of *file*.

EOR Abbreviation for end of *run*.

EOT Abbreviation for *end-of-transmission character*.

EPROM 1. Acronym for erasable *programmable read-only memory*. A read-only memory that may be both programmed and erased in the *field*[2]. Erasure is often carried out in strong ultraviolet light. 2. Acronym for electrically programmable read-only memory (electrically erasable).

equality Synonymous with *Exclusive-Nor operation*.

equal zero indicator An *indicator* which is set if the result of a calculation or test is zero; the indicator can then be tested by a *branch instruction*.

equipment failure Any *hardware* fault that prevents the completion of a job.

equivalence A logical relationship in which two statements are equivalent if they are both true or both false.

equivalent binary digits The number of *bits* necessary to represent each *character* of a set of characters by a unique *binary number*. For example, there are twenty-six characters in an alphabet set, and five equivalent binary digits are therefore necessary, since there are five bits in 11010, the binary notation for 26.

erasable programmable ROM ◊ *EPROM*.

erasable storage Any *storage* medium in which a location can be re-used because new data overwrites data previously occupying that location.

erase To replace data in a *storage* medium by a uniform code representing null data.
Also known as letter out or rubout.

erase character Synonymous with *ignore character*.

error Any condition in which the actual results of an operation deviate from the correct results. There is an implication that an error is due to an acceptable, identifiable cause such as rounding (◊ *round off*), while a mistake is human but not acceptable. Perhaps euphemistically, mistakes by *operators*[1] and *programmers*[1] are known as operator errors, programmer errors.

error character Synonymous with *ignore character*.

error-checking code A general term embracing all *error-correcting codes* and *error-detecting codes*.

error code The marking of a particular *error* by means of a *character* or code. The error code can be printed out to indicate that an error has occurred, or can be associated on a *storage* device with an item of data which is in error so that the item may be ignored or corrected when the data is subsequently processed.

error-correcting code An *error-detecting code* designed to assist not only in the recognition of the fact that an error has occurred, but also in the recognition of what the correct code should have been.

error-correction routine A *routine* for the detection and correction of errors on *data files*.

error-detecting code A *code* in which the representation of each *character* conforms to specific rules of construction. These rules ensure that certain combinations of the elements out of which the set of characters is constructed are not valid: these combinations can be recognized and rejected as errors.
Also known as self-checking code.

error diagnostics The process of checking *source language statements* for errors during compilation, and the printing of error messages identifying any errors discovered.

error interrupts An *interrupt* which occurs as a result of a *program* or *hardware* error.

error list A list produced by a compiler showing incorrect or invalid *instructions* in a *source program*.

error range The range of values for an item of data which will cause an *error* condition if the item value falls within the range.

error rate In *data transmission*, the ratio of the total number of transmission errors to the total volume of data transmitted.

error routine A *routine* which is entered on the detection of an error. The routine may output an *error message*, attempt to correct the error, repeat the process which caused the error or perform any other specified action.

error tape A *magnetic tape* on to which *errors* are written for subsequent listing and analysis.

escape character A *character* which indicates that the following character belongs to a different *character set* from that of the preceding characters.

ETP Abbreviation for *electrical tough pitch*.

even parity check A *parity check* in which the number of ones (or zeroes) in a group of *binary digits* is expected to be even. Contrasted with *odd parity check*.

event 1. An occurrence which affects an item on a *data file*; a transaction. 2. In *critical path analysis*, an occurrence which ends one *activity*[2] and begins another.

except gate   Synonymous with *Exclusive-Or* element.

excess fifty   A *binary code* in which a number n is represented by the binary equivalent of $n+50$.

excess three code   A *binary code* in which a number n is represented by the binary equivalent of $n+3$.

exchangeable disk store   (EDS) A *backing store* device which uses *magnetic disks* loaded in a *disk drive*; the operator can replace capsules of, for example, six disks during operation.

exchange buffering   A *buffering* system which allows system buffer areas and user buffer areas to be exchanged, eliminating the need for movement of data items in *main memory*.

Exclusive-Nor   A *Boolean operation* on two *operands* (p and q), the *result* (r) being given in the following table:

Operands		Result
p	q	r
0	0	0
1	0	1
0	1	1
1	1	0

Also known as bi-conditional operation, equality, non-equivalence, except.

Exclusive-Or   A *Boolean operation* on two *operands* (p and q), the result (r) being given in the following table:

Operands		Result
p	q	r
1	1	1
1	0	0
0	1	0
0	0	1

Also known as distance, diversity, except gate, exjunction, symmetric difference.

execute 1. To perform the operations specified by a *routine* or *instruction*. 2. To cause, by some external action such as setting a *console switch*, an instruction to be performed.

execute cycle Synonymous with *execute phase*.

execute phase That part of the *control cycle*[1] in which, after it has been *accessed*, an *instruction* is performed.

Also known as execute cycle.

execution The running of *object code* in order to perform a *program*'s function.

execution time The time taken to complete the cycle of events required to *execute* an *instruction*.

executive program A number of complex *routines* which reside in *main memory* and which control the *loading*[2] and *execution* of other *programs*. Executive programs have a close interaction with the *hardware* facilities of a computer and are often described as *middleware*, *intimate software* or *systems software*. ⊗ *operating system*.

exhaustivity The number of *keywords* assigned to a *record* in a file in an information retrieval system.

exit The final *instruction* in a *routine*, usually a *branch* from the routine into another part of the *program* or into a *control* routine.

exjunction Synonymous with *Exclusive-Or* operation.

expansion cascading Moving from a fine level of detail to increasingly broad levels. Contrasted with *reduction cascading*, or moving from broad levels to increasing detail.

exponent The power to which a quantity is raised, i.e. the number of times it is to be a factor to produce a product. For example, in the expression 2^{36} the exponent is 36.

expression One or more symbols to which a meaning is assigned.

Extended Binary Coded Decimal Interchange Code ⊘ *EBCDIC*.

extended time-scale A time-scale in which a *time-scale factor* of greater than one is used in processing.

extension memory Synonymous with *external store*.

exterior label A label placed on the outside of a *reel*[3]. Contrasted with *interior label*.

external memory Synonymous with *external store*.

external store *Store* which is under the control of, but not necessarily permanently connected to, a *central processor*; can be plugged into a *mother board*.

Also known as extension memory, external memory.

extract   1. To remove a selected part or sub-set from an item or set of items of information. 2. That part of the set which is so removed.

extract instruction   An *instruction* which will move selected *extracts*[2] into a specified *location*. ⟡ *masking*.

extractor   Synonymous with *mask*.

facsimile The process of scanning an image and converting it into transmission signals which are used at a receiving station to produce a recorded copy of the original.
Also known as fax.

factor Either of the *operands* in a multiplication operation.

factorial The product of positive integers from 1 up to and including a given integer; for example, factorial 6 is the product of $1 \times 2 \times 3 \times 4 \times 5 \times 6$, or 720.

fade The fluctuation in intensity of any or all components of a received signal.

fail safe 1. Descriptive of a system which is able to close down in a controlled way in the event of a serious *failure*, although some deterioration in performance is expected. 2. Synonymous with *fail soft*, with the implication of protecting data against loss.

fail soft Descriptive of a system which is able to close down in the event of a serious *failure* with no loss of data and no more than an interruption of processing until the failure is corrected. The term is sometimes used interchangeably with *fail safe*, but the implication is that fail-safe systems halt less gently and with more damage than fail-soft systems, which parachute to easy landings.
Also known as soft-fail.

failure A disruption caused by a defect or malfunction in *hardware* or *software*.

failure logging The automatic recording of *failures* which can be detected by *program*, allowing corrective procedures to be attempted.

failure rate A measure of the number of a specified type or class of *failures* occurring in a specific period.

failure recovery Resumption of a system after a *failure*; perhaps after correction of the failure or perhaps after the system has been *reconfigured* to avoid use of a troublesome component.

false drop Synonymous with *false retrieval*.

false error The signalling of an *error* when no error exists.

false retrieval An unwanted item of data, retrieved as a result of an error in specification of selection criteria.

Also known as false drop.

farad   A measurement of the ability of two insulated bodies to hold a static charge equal to one coulomb at a potential difference of one volt between the two bodies, or one coulomb per volt. Most capacitors need to be measured in a rather smaller unit, hence the microfarad and picofarad.

fast time-scale   An operation scale in which the *time-scale factor* is less than one. Contrasted with *extended time-scale*.

fault   The failure of any physical component of a system, *hardware* or *software*.

fault time   Synonymous with *down time*.

fault-tolerant   A *program* or system which may continue to operate successfully in spite of a *fault* or faults. Related to *graceful degradation*.

fax   Synonymous with *facsimile*.

FDM   Abbreviation for *frequency division multiplexing*.

feasibility study   Initial research into the suitability and capability of possible solutions to a problem, usually resulting in estimates of time-scales, costs and benefits of an outline solution.

feed   1. To cause data to be entered into a computer, with the implication of doing so by means of *punched cards*, *paper tape*, or other medium rather than by *direct data entry*. 2. A device for causing data to be entered.

feedback   The return of some part of output to be used as input in a *closed-loop* system, usually to provide information about the condition under control for comparison with a target value.

FEP   Abbreviation for *front-end processor*.

ferrite core   A small piece of ring-shaped magnetic material, capable of receiving and holding an electromagnetic charge, used in *core* store.

fetch   1. The part of *instruction execution* in which the next instruction *address* is located and the next *storage location* is determined and the contents fetched. 2. Synonymous with *retrieve*.

field   1. A specified part of a *record*, containing a unit of information; for example, a personnel record might contain fields for personnel number, name, job title, age, date of joining, gross pay. 2. On a user's premises; away from an original manufacturer. When a unit is capable of being enhanced in the field, it can be enhanced on site, without the need to return the unit to the supplier.

field length The number of *characters* or *words* in a *field* or a *fixed-length record*.

FIFO Acronym for first in, first out. 1. A discipline for use of communication lines. 2. Data written in a FIFO *memory* is stored in the next available *location*, and a *read* operation advances the process to the next unread *word* in memory. Once the read causes the advance, the previous word cannot be read again.

FIFO queue A first in, first out queue in which the item which has been longest in the queue receives attention first.

file An organized collection of related *records*. The records on a file may be related by a specific purpose, format, or data source, and the records may or may not be arranged in *sequence*. A file may be made up of *records*, *fields*, *words*, *bytes*, *characters* or *bits*.

file activity ratio The ratio of the number of *records* or other file element for which a *transaction*[1] occurs during a given number of *runs* to the number of records or other file elements in the file.

file conversion The process of converting *files* of data either from one medium to another or from one format to another. In either case the process is usually more hazardous than expected.

file extent A specific area of a *file* consisting of contiguous *tracks* on a file *storage* medium.
Also known as file section.

file identification A *code*[2] in the form of a *label* or *tag* devised to identify a *file*. The objective is to ensure that there is no confusion between files containing different data, and to allow *programs* *reading* and *writing* files to check that the correct files are input and output. ⟡ *file label*, *tape label*.

file label A type of *file identification*; the first *record* or *block* in a file is a set of *characters* unique to the file. Information in the file label may include a description of the file contents, the file *generation number*, and, if the file is on *magnetic tape*, the *reel*[3] number and the date written to tape.
Also known as header label.

file layout A description of the method of organization and contents of a *file*.

file maintenance 1. Synonymous with *updating*. 2. Changing the contents of a *file* by the addition, deletion or correction of *records*, but distinguished from updating by the implication of caretaking to ensure that files are in good order and economically organized, while updating reflects real change in the data recorded on the files.

83

file manager A *routine*, usually part of an *operating system*, which carries out such services as file access control, *file protection* and cataloguing.

file name The set of *characters* used to identify and describe a *file* in a *file label*.

file name extension *Characters* added to the *file name* to identify the type of data held in the file.

file organization The method used for mapping *records* on to a physical *storage* medium. The method chosen may require a specific method of file access such as *serial* or *random access*.

file print A *printout* of the complete contents of a file, usually made for the process of file checking or *debugging*.

file processing The operations connected with the creation and use of *files*, including *creation*, validation (⟡ *validate*), *comparison*, *collating*, *sorting* and *merging*. Routines used for file processing are known as utilities or *utility programs*.

file protection Precautions taken to prevent accidental *overwriting* of data *files* before they are released for use in another system. File protection can be by *hardware*, e.g. through the use of *file-protection rings* on *magnetic tape*, or by causing a program to check *file labels*.

file-protection ring A detachable ring which is fitted to the hub of a *magnetic tape* reel to indicate the status of the reel. Such rings can be write-permit rings (which ensure that data can be *written* to a file only if the ring is fitted) or write-inhibit rings (in which case data cannot be written to the tape when the ring is fitted).

file purging The erasure of the contents of a *file*, perhaps as a result of reaching a *purge date*.

file reconstitution The re-creation of a *file* which has been corrupted during system *failure* or as a result of, for example, a fire. The process may involve the use of a file of *transactions*[2] in updating a previous generation (⟡ *generation number*) of the file.

file recovery Reorganizing a *file* after the interruption of processing by a system *failure*, ensuring that the file contents reflect *transactions* received during the system failure period. ⟡ *file reconstitution*, which is necessary when greater disruption has occurred.

file section Synonymous with *file extent*.

file set A collection of *files* forming a unit and stored consecutively on a *magnetic disk* unit.

file store The *files* required by an *operating system*, usually stored on a *backing store*.

fill To complete a *fixed-length record* with useless data which does not distort the existing data in the *field*[1].

film ◊ *thick-film memory* or *thin-film memory*.

filter Synonymous with *mask*.

firmware 1. A *program blown* into *ROM*; logic which has been permanently hard-wired (◊ *hard-wired logic*); distinguished from *hardware* only by the fact that the functions performed were once carried out by *software*. 2. Software which interacts intimately with hardware carrying out essential systems software functions.

first-level address Synonymous with *absolute address*.

fixed block length The length of *blocks* of data with a constant number of *words* or *characters*, required either because of *hardware* limitations, or determined by *program*.

fixed field The organization of *fields* in *records* in such a way that fields containing similar information in each record are located in the same relative position within the record and are the same length.

fixed-length record A *record* whose size in *words* or *characters* is constant. This may be because of *hardware* requirements, or be determined by *program*.

fixed-point arithmetic A method of performing arithmetical calculations without regard to the position of the *radix point*, treating the numbers as integers for the purpose of calculation. The relative position of the point is controlled during calculations by ensuring that the digits of all numbers are in the correct relative positions.

fixed-point part That part of a *floating-point number* which indicates the number of times that the number base with the *exponent* is to be multiplied.
Also known as coefficient.

fixed-point representation A *number system* in which a number is represented by a single set of *digits*, the value of the number depending on the position of the digits. For fractional numbers the *radix point* is located at a fixed predetermined position. ◊ *positional notation*, *floating-point representation*.

flag An additional item of information added to a data item which provides information about the data item itself. A flag is usually one *bit* and is the software equivalent of a *flip-flop*.
Also known as sentinel.

flag event A condition which causes a *flag* to be set; for example, the identification of an error, resulting in an error flag.

flip-flop A bistable device or circuit which assumes one of two possible states (0 or 1); the nature of the state is reversed on receipt of an input signal.

Also known as binary pair, bistable circuit, bistable multivibrator, Eccles Jordan circuit, toggle.

flippy   Synonymous with *floppy disk*.

float   To add the *origin* to all *relative addresses* in a *program* in order to determine how much *memory* the program will occupy.

float factor   Synonymous with *origin*.

floating address   Synonymous with *relative address*.

floating-point arithmetic   Arithmetical calculations based on numbers expressed using *floating-point representation*. The position of the *radix point* does not depend on the relative position of the digits in the numbers (as it does in *fixed-point arithmetic*) because the two parts of the floating-point number determine the absolute value of the number. The use of floating-point arithmetic allows numbers to be stored more economically and in wider ranges of magnitudes.

floating-point number   A number expressed in *floating-point representation*.

floating-point package   *Software* which enables a computer to perform *floating-point arithmetic*.

floating-point representation   A *number system* in which a number is represented by two sets of *digits*, known as the *fixed-point part* and the *exponent*. (The fixed-point part is also known as the fractional part, significant digits, coefficient, argument and mantissa.) If a number n is represented by a fixed-point part a and an exponent b, then $n = a.r^b$, where r is the *radix* of the number system. Contrasted with *fixed-point representation*.

flop   *Floating-point* operation.

floppy   Synonymous with *floppy disk*.

floppy disk   A *magnetic disk* which can be readily handled in non-controlled *environments*[1]; relatively inexpensive. The name derives from the disk's comparative malleability.

Also known as diskette, flippy, floppy.

flops   Number of *floating-point* operations per second.

flow   A sequence of events involved in the solution of a problem, often represented in a *flowchart*.

flowchart   The diagrammatic representation of a *flow*, usually drawn with conventional symbols representing different types of event and their relationships. ◊ *flowchart symbols*, *program flowchart*, *systems flowchart*.

Also known as flow diagram.

flowchart symbols Conventional diagrammatic representations of different events which are shown on a *flowchart*. A number of standard symbols have been adopted, but changes in computing tend to overtake the standardization process.

flow diagram Synonymous with *flowchart*.

flow direction The direction on a *flowchart* from one event to another. Distinguishing between antecedent and successor event may be by means of arrows or by the convention that *flowlines* connecting antecedent to successor flow from top to bottom and left to right of a page.

flowline A line drawn on a *flowchart* to connect antecedent event to a successor event. ◊ *flow direction*.

flow-process diagram Synonymous with *systems flowchart*.

flutter A recurring speed variation of relatively low frequency in a moving medium.

flyback The time taken by a spot on a *terminal screen* to move from the end of a line to the beginning of the next.

forbidden character A certain combination of *bits* which can be recognized by an *error-detecting code* as illegal.

force To intervene in the operation of a *program*, usually by *executing* a *branch instruction* to transfer control to another part of the *routine*. Forcing is usually carried out to by-pass an *error* condition which has caused the program to come to a halt, or to terminate a run by forcing entry to the end-of-run routine.

foregrounding Synonymous with *foreground processing*.

foreground processing A phrase to be used with caution as it has two directly contradictory meanings, both in common use. 1. In *multiprogramming*, high-priority processing which takes precedence (as a result of *interrupts*[1]) over *background processing*. 2. Low-priority processing over which background processing takes precedence. 3. In a *time sharing* environment, processing which makes use of *on-line* facilities.

foreground program A *program* which requires *foreground processing*.

format The specified arrangement of data, e.g. the layout of a printed document, the arrangement of the parts of a computer *instruction*, the arrangement of data in a *record*.

format effector Synonymous with *layout character*.

form flash Synonymous with *form overlay*.

form overlay Displaying on a *terminal* a stored form, either to assist in explaining the data also displayed or to assist in input. Also known as form flash.

form stop A device which automatically stops a *printer* when the paper has run out.

FORTRAN A *high-level language, problem orientated* for scientific and mathematical use, written in a combination of algebraic formulae and English statements in a readable form. The name is an acronym for FORmula TRANslation.

forward bias A voltage applied to a p-n crystal so that the positive terminal is applied to the p section and the negative to the n section. ◊ *p-type, n-type*.

forward current The current which flows through a semiconductor junction when a *forward bias* is applied.

four-address instruction An *instruction* whose *address* part consists of four addresses, usually two *operand* addresses, the address of the destination of the result of the operation and the address of the next instruction to be performed.

four-wire channel A circuit capable of transmitting and receiving at the same time by the use of two separate and distinct paths in each direction.

fractional part Synonymous with *fixed-point part*.

frame 1. An image in a *display* system. 2. The data needed to create such an image, while the data is held in *memory* or *backing store*. 3. The time period needed to transmit a specific set of *bits*.

frequency The rate of repetition of a periodically recurring signal, usually measured in cycles per second. One Hertz (Hz) is one cycle per second, a kiloHertz (kHz) is one thousand cycles per second, and a megaHertz (MHz) is one million cycles per second.

frequency band The range within which it is acceptable for the *frequency* of a signal to vary.

frequency division multiplexing (FDM) The partitioning of a limited bandwidth communication channel into lower speed channels which utilize an assigned part of the frequency spectrum for transmitting *binary* data signals.

FROM Acronym for *fusable read-only memory*.

front-end processor (FEP) A *central processor* interposed between input channels and another processor, and having the function of preprocessing data before it is input to a larger processor, thus saving time on the larger machine. ◊ *concentrator*.

full adder Synonymous with *adder*.

full duplex   Synonymous with *duplex*.

full subtracter   Synonymous with *subtracter*.

function   The *operation* specified in an *instruction*.

functional unit   A series of *elements* which together perform a single computer *operation*, e.g. multiplication or addition.

function code   The part of a computer *instruction* which specifies the *operation* to be performed.

function table   In *table* look-up techniques, a table which consists of two or more sets of information arranged so that an item in one set provides a cross-reference to items in the other sets.

fusable read-only memory   (FROM) *Read-only memory* which is programmed by the *blowing* of fuse links. Once fused, FROMs cannot be altered or corrected.

G

gain   The ratio of the strength of an output signal from a circuit to the strength of the original input signal.

gap   The interval between *blocks* of data on a *magnetic tape* necessary to enable the medium to be stopped and started between reading or writing. ⟡ *interblock gap*.

gap character   A *character* present in a *string* such as a *word*, for some purpose other than to represent data or *instructions*, e.g. a *parity bit*.

gap digit   A *digit* present in a *word* for some purpose other than to represent data or *instructions*, e.g. a *parity bit*.

gap scatter   The deviation from correct alignment of the magnetic *read/write heads* for the parallel *tracks* on a *magnetic tape*.

garbage   Meaningless and unwanted data. The data may be meaningless because of errors or may be data left in *store* by a previous unrelated job.

garbage collection   The rearrangement of the contents of *store* and the elimination of unwanted data in order to reclaim space for new data. ⟡ *garbage*.

gate   An electronic switch, used in microprocessors to refer to any circuit which may have more than one *input signal* but only one *output signal*. In this sense, synonymous with *logical element*.

gathering, data   ⟡ *data collection*.

gather write   The process of *writing* a *block* of data composed of logical *records* from non-continuous areas of *store*. ⟡ *scatter read*.

generate   To use a *generator* to produce a *program* or *coding* automatically.

generated address   An *address* produced as a result of *instructions* within a *program* for use subsequently by that program.
Also known as synthetic address.

generated error   A total error produced by using operands which are not accurate (⟡ *accuracy*), e.g. using rounded numbers.

generating program   Synonymous with *generator*.

generating routine   Synonymous with *generator*.

generation number   A number forming part of the *file label* on a *reel*[3] of *magnetic tape*, which identifies the amendment level or copy number of the file. Each time amendment data is written to a magnetic tape file a new copy of the file is created containing all the valid amendments. This new reel carries the same *file name* as that carried by the reel that has just been amended, but the two reels are different generations of the same file and therefore bear different generation numbers. ⟂ *grandfather tape*.

generator A *routine* which produces a *program* to carry out a specific version of a general operation; it does so by completing a predetermined skeleton program with the details or parameters of the specific application. A generator is similar to a *compiler* in that *source*² *statements* are converted into a program, but differs in that only programs of a specific type are produced, e.g. *sort* generator, *report generator*.
Also known as generating program, generating routine, program generator.

gibberish total Synonymous with *hash total*.

giga- A prefix denoting 10^9, or one thousand million.

GIGO Acronym for 'garbage in garbage out'; the principle that the results produced by unreliable data are also unreliable.

global Pertaining to an item defined in one *routine* of a *program* and used in at least one other routine. Contrasted with *local*.

graceful degradation The process of undergoing *failure* in such a way that limited operation can continue. ⟂ *fail soft* and *resilience*¹.

grandfather tape A copy of a *magnetic tape file* which, since the copy was made, has twice undergone an updating cycle. Each of the resulting copies (original, first copy, second copy) represents a generation which may be used in reconstituting the file in the event of serious damage to the current version. The three are called respectively 'grandfather', 'father' and 'son', each being identified by a *generation number*.

graphic 1. Representational or pictorial, contrasted, in a computer context, with textual. ⟂ *graphics*. 2. A symbol produced for graphic representation.
Also known as graphical symbol.

graphic character A character used for *graphic* representation, e.g. a group of symbols on a *terminal* display screen.

graphic data structure The logical arrangement of *digital* data representing *graphic* data for graphic display.

graphic display resolution 1. The number of lines and characters per line able to be shown on a *terminal screen*. 2. The number of *pels* of a screen.

graphic panel   A device which displays the state of a *process control* operation in the form of lights, dials, etc.

graphics   The methods and techniques of processing data to result in displays of pictorial representation; embraces *interactive* graphics.

graphic solution   A solution to a problem provided by means of graphs or diagrams rather than printed figures or text.

graphic symbol   Synonymous with *graphic*².

graph plotter   ◊ *plotter*.

graunch   An unexpectedly damaging *error*.

Gray code   A code in which the binary representations of the numbers 0–9 are given in the following table:

Decimal	Gray
0	0000
1	0001
2	0011
3	0010
4	0110
5	0111
6	0101
7	0100
8	1100
9	1101

Also known as cyclic code.

group mark   A *character* used to indicate the end of a group of characters in *store*; the group itself is usually a logical *record* and processed as a unit of data.

Also known as group marker.

group marker   Synonymous with *group mark*.

group poll   To *poll* a number of devices forming a subset of available devices.

guard band   A frequency band between two *channels* of a *data transmission* device, left unused in order to prevent interference between channels.

guard signal   A signal which permits values to be read only when the values are not subject to *ambiguity error*.

gulp   A small group of *binary digits* consisting of several *bytes*, and treated as a unit.

H

half adder A device or logic element forming part of an *adder* and able to receive two inputs (*augend* and either *addend* or *carry*) and deliver two outputs, *sum* and carry.

Also known as one-digit adder.

half adjust To round a number in such a way that the least significant digit determines whether a one is to be added to the next least significant digit. After this adjustment, the original least significant digit is omitted. The rule for determination is that if the least significant digit is less than half the *radix*, it is simply omitted; if it is half or more, then a one is added to the next least significant digit, the original is omitted and all *carries* are propagated.

half-duplex A method of communication between two points in which signals may be transmitted and received but in only one direction at a time, with or without an *interrupt*[1] feature enabling the receiving station to interrupt the sending station.

Also known as either-way operation.

half-duplex channel A *channel* which allows signals to be transmitted and received, but in only one direction at a time.

half intensity A *terminal screen* characteristic which allows specified characters to be displayed at half the intensity or brightness of the standard character.

half-word A continuous *string* of *characters* making up half a *word* and capable of being *addressed* as a unit.

halt The condition which occurs when a *program* sequence comes to a stop. This can be the result of a *halt instruction*, or because of an unexpected halt or *interrupt*. The program can usually continue after a halt, unless it is a *drop-dead halt*.

halt, dead ◊ *drop-dead halt*.

halt, drop-dead ◊ *drop-dead halt*.

halt instruction An *instruction* to cause a *halt*.

Also known as stop code, stop instruction.

Hamming code An *error-checking code* named after its inventor, R. W. Hamming. Each *character* has a minimum Hamming *signal distance* from every other character in the code.

Hamming distance Synonymous with *signal distance*.

handshake   A communications *interface* preceding transmission, in which a signal is requested, received and acknowledged. This procedure obviates ignored or overlapping signalling between devices.

hands-off operation   Synonymous with *closed shop*.

hands-on operation   Synonymous with *open shop*.

hang-up   An unexpected *halt* in a *program* sequence, caused by a program *error*.

hard copy   A document produced in a tangible form suitable for human beings to read produced at the same time as information is produced for a transient *display* or in *machine code*.

hard error   A fault, usually concerned with a *hardware* malfunction, which can be readily diagnosed and to some extent predicted (e.g. the failure of a component at the end of its expected life). Contrasted with *soft error*.

hardware   The physical units making up a *computer system*[1] – the apparatus as opposed to the *programs*. Contrasted with *software* and *firmware*.

hardware check   A *check* carried out by *hardware* to detect errors in the transmission of data by circuits within a computer, e.g. *parity check* performed by hardware.
Also known as automatic check (when applied to hardware), built-in check.

hard-wired logic   Logic designs using a number of interconnected integrated circuits wired for specific operations and unalterable as compared with, for example, programmable *read-only memory* circuits, which are alterable to change the purpose of their operation.

hash   Meaningless or unwanted information present in a storage medium, perhaps to comply with *hardware* requirements for a minimum *block* size. ♢ *hash total*.

hash total   An addition of all values in a *field* or area of a *file* where the total has no informational significance but serves a control purpose, e.g. a total of payroll numbers.
Also known as check sum, gibberish total.

head   A device used to read, record or erase data on a magnetic *storage* medium such as *magnetic tape*, *disk* or *drum*. The device is typically an electromagnet, such as a *read/write head*.

head, combined   ♢ *read/write head*.

head crash   Damage caused to a *magnetic disk* surface as a result of impact by the *read/write head*.

header A group of data items placed at the head of one or more sets of data and containing an identifying *key* for these following sets. Sometimes the header will contain *control data* or routing of data common to the following sets.

header label A block of data at the start of a *magnetic tape file*. The block contains descriptive information to identify the file, such as *file name, reel*[3] *sequence number, file generation number,* retention period, date written.

Also known as file label.

head gap The distance between a read or write head (⬦ *read/write head*) and the surface of the recording medium.

heading A sequence of *characters* preceding the text of a message, representing routing and destination data in *data transmission*.

head, playback ⬦ *read/write head.*

head, reading ⬦ *read/write head.*

head, record ⬦ *write head.*

head, writing ⬦ *write head.*

Hertz (Hz) A unit of frequency (named after Heinrich Hertz, a nineteenth-century German physicist) equal to one cycle per second.

hesitation A brief automatic suspension of a main program in order to carry out all or part of another operation, e.g. a fast transfer of data to or from a *peripheral unit*.

heuristic approach An exploratory method of problem solving which uses successive evaluations of trial and error to approach a final result. Contrasted with *algorithmic* approach.

heuristic program A *program* which solves a problem by *heuristic approach*.

hex Abbreviation for *hexadecimal notation*.

hexadecimal notation (hex) A notation of numbers to the base (*radix*) of sixteen. The ten decimal digits 0 to 9 are used, and in addition six more digits, usually a, b, c, d, e, and f, to represent ten, eleven, twelve, thirteen, fourteen and fifteen as single characters. One *byte* can be encoded in two symbols and hex is therefore much used by microprocessor users.

hex pad A keyboard designed for input to a microprocessor in *hexadecimal notation*.

hidden line A *line*[2] in a graphic display which is obscured from view in a projection of a three-dimensional object. The hidden line is nevertheless represented in the graphic structure so that it can be revealed when, for example, the image is rotated on the screen.

Hg delay line   Synonymous with *mercury delay line*.

high-level language   A *programming* language which allows its users to write *instructions* in a notation (problem-orientated or procedure-orientated) with which they are familiar, rather than in a *machine code*. Each *statement* in a high-level language corresponds to several *machine code* instructions. Contrasted with *low-level language*. See also *ADA, ALGOL, BASIC, COBOL, CORAL, FORTRAN, LISP, Microcobol, PASCAL, PL/M, PL/1, SNOBOL*.

high order   Relating to the significance attached to a number; e.g. in the numeric representation of twenty-seven as 27, the 2 is of a higher order than the 7, since it represents tens rather than units. In describing a *binary word*, therefore, reference can be made to the high-order *bits*.

highpass   Relating to the performance of a circuit which allows the passage of high-frequency signals and *attenuates* low-frequency signals.

high-performance equipment   Equipment which produces output *signals* of sufficiently high quality to allow these signals to be transmitted on telephone or teleprinter circuits.

high-speed bus   ⬦ *bus*.

high-speed carry   A *carry* into a column which results in a carry out of that column, by-passing the normal adding circuit when the new carry is generated. Also known as a ripple-through carry or, where appropriate, standing-on-nines carry. When the normal adding circuit is used in such a case, it is called a *cascaded carry*.

highway   Synonymous with *bus*.

hit   The finding of a matching *record*; e.g. in a *retrieval* system, an answer found when the *label* of a stored item matches the search *key*; or, in *file maintenance*, the matching of a detail record with a *master record*.

hold   To retain data in one *storage device* after transferring it to another storage device or to another location in the same device. The data is held because it is still needed for some other operation in the program. Contrasted with *clear*.

hold facility   The ability to allow interruption of the operation of a computer in such a way that the values of the *variables* at the time of interruption are not altered; this allows computation to continue when the interruption ceases.

holding beam   A diffuse spray of electrons in a *cathode ray tube*, used for *refreshing*; electrons which have dissipated after being stored on the surface can be refreshed by a holding beam.

holding gun The source of a spray of electrons forming a *holding beam*.

hole A freely moving positive charge in a *doped* semiconductor crystal.

Hollerith card A *punched card* in which information is punched using the *Hollerith code*.

Hollerith code A *punched-card code* invented by Dr Herman Hollerith in 1888 in which holes in the top three positions in a column have a zoning significance and are combined with holes in the other positions to represent alphabetic, numeric and special characters.

hologram A recording of an image distributed over a film surface as a result of splitting a laser beam, producing an optical interference. The image can be recovered and focused in free space or on a screen. Holograms can be used for data *storage*, with extremely high *packing densities*.

home The starting position for the *cursor* on a *terminal screen*, usually in the top left-hand corner of the screen

homeostasis The dynamic state of a system where input and output are exactly balanced, so that there is no change.

home record The first *record* in a *file* of *chained records*.

host computer The controlling machine in a multiple computer activity, perhaps with *front-end processors*.

hot chassis A *terminal* with its *chassis* connected to one side of a power line, so that the chassis itself provides the earth or ground. Direct input of a video signal to a hot chassis constitutes a safety hazard and an *RF modulator* is desirable.

housekeeping *Routines* which directly contribute to the successful operation of a system but which are not directly concerned with the solution of a problem. Housekeeping functions might include the setting of initial or *entry conditions*, *clearing* areas of *store*, performing any standard preliminary operations required by *input* or *output devices* such as writing *labels* to *magnetic tape* and performing standard *input/output operations*.

hub The hole in the middle of a *reel*² of *magnetic tape*. The hub fits over the *capstan* when the reel is mounted on a *tape deck*.

hybrid computer A computing system which combines *analog* and *digital* devices.

Hz Abbreviation for *Hertz*.

IAL Abbreviation for International Algebraic Language, later developed into *ALGOL*.

IC Abbreviation for *integrated circuit*.

icand Abbreviation for *multiplicand*.

identification A *label* consisting of a coded name identifying a unit of data; e.g. a *file name*.

identification division In *COBOL* one of the four divisions of a *source program*; the division in which the programmer specifies the identities and formats of the items of data to be processed by his program.

identifier A *label* which identifies a *file* or a particular *location* in store. ⊘ *file identification*.

identify To assign a *label* to a *file* or data or to an item of data held in *store*.

identity element A *logical element* which provides one *output* signal from two *input* signals. The output signal will be 1 if, and only if, the two input signals are alike, both 1 or both 0.

ier Abbreviation for *multiplier*.

if-and-only-if operation Synonymous with *equivalence* operation.

If-Then operation Synonymous with *conditional implication operation*.

ignore Synonymous with *ignore character*.

ignore character A character which either causes an action to be inhibited, or is itself ignored.
Also known as erase character, error character.

illegal character A group of *bits* which does not represent any of the valid symbols in the *character set* of the system.

illegal instruction An *instruction* not recognized by the *instruction set* of a computer and thus incapable of being *executed*.

image A copy of an area of *store* located in another part of store or in a different *storage* medium. ⊘ *hologram*.

image sensor Synonymous with *charge couple device*.

immediate address The *address* part of an *instruction* which is used by the instruction itself.
Also known as zero-level address.

immediate processing Synonymous with *demand processing*.

imperative macro instructions *Macroinstructions* which are converted into *object program* instructions; contrasted with *declarative macro* instructions which result in the *compiler* performing a particular action.

imperative statements *Instructions* in a *symbolic language program* which are converted into the actual *machine-code* instructions of an *object program*. Action *instructions* of a symbolic program that are converted into machine language instructions of an object program.

implication Synonymous with *conditional implication operation*.

impulse Synonymous with *pulse*.

inclusion Synonymous with *conditional implication operation*.

Inclusive-Nor operation Synonymous with *Nor operation*.

Inclusive-Or operation Synonymous with *Or operation*.

increment 1. A quantity which is added to another quantity. 2. To add a quantity to another quantity, e.g. to advance a number *stored* in a *register*.

incremental computer A *computer* which represents as absolute values the changes to *variables* rather than the variables themselves.

indexed address An *address* modified (⟡ *modifier*) by the contents of a modifier, or index word.

index hole A hole cut in a *floppy disk* to indicate the start of the first *sector*.

indexing slot Synonymous with *polarizing slot*.

index register A *register* used for containing a *modifier*.
Also known as b-line, b-register, b-store.

index sequential file A *file* on a *random access storage device* in which the *address* of a *record* on a physical file is identified on an index which contains the record *key*.

index word Synonymous with *modifier*.

indicator A device or signal which may be set in accordance with a specified condition or the result of a process or event. An indicator may be tested by *program* and the result of this test can initiate an appropriate action.
Also known as alteration switch.

indirect addressing A method of *addressing* in which the *address* part of an *instruction* refers to another *location* which contains another address. This further address may specify an *operand* or *operator* or yet another address.

Also known as multi-level addressing.

inequivalence   Synonymous with *Exclusive-Or*.

infix notation   A *notation* for representing *logical operations* in which the *operator* is written between the *operands*, e.g. A&B where & represents the operation 'and'. Contrasted with *prefix notation*.

information   Data so assembled and presented that it is given meaning. (The distinction between data and information was once carefully preserved, but now no longer seems important.)

information channel   The *hardware* used in a *data transmission* link between two *terminals*, including *modulator*, *demodulator*, and any error-detection equipment required. A channel may involve transmission by telegraph or telephone lines or by a radio or satellite link.

information feedback   A *data transmission* control method, in which data received at a *terminal* is re-transmitted to the sending terminal for automatic checking. ⌀ *feedback*.

inherited error   An *error* in a result or intermediate result of a previous stage of processing, carried over to the current operation.

inhibit   To prevent a *signal* from occurring, or a specific operation from being performed.

inhibit pulse   A pulse applied to a magnetic cell to prevent a *drive*[2] impulse from reversing the flux of that cell.

initial address   The address assigned to the initial *location* of a *program*.

Also known as program origin (but ⌀ *origin*).

initial condition   Synonymous with *entry condition*.

initial error   The *error* represented by the difference between the actual value of a data unit and the value used at the start of processing.

initial instructions   A *routine* in *memory* whose purpose is to facilitate *loading*[2].

Also known as initial orders.

initialization   A process carried out at the beginning of a *program* to test that all *indicators* and constants are set to prescribed conditions.

initial orders   Synonymous with *initial instructions*.

in-line processing   Synonymous with *demand processing*.

in-line subroutine   A *subroutine* directly inserted into a *program* and which must be recopied each time it is required; contrasted with a subroutine which can be entered from the main program each time it is required.

input 1. To transfer *data* or *instructions* from a *peripheral unit* into *memory*. 2. Data or instructions which are so transferred. 3. The *signals* applied to circuits to effect such a transfer. (It is therefore possible, if inelegant, to speak of inputting input by means of an input.)

input area The area in *main memory* into which data from a *backing store* or *peripheral unit* is transferred before being distributed to appropriate *work areas* for processing.

Also known as input block, input storage.

input block 1. Synonymous with *input area*. 2. A *block* of data being transferred into an *input area*.

input device Equipment which provides a vehicle for communication between people and computers by allowing *data* and *instructions* to be entered into *main memory*. Such devices may accept data already converted into *punched cards*, *paper tape*, magnetic ink (◇ *magnetic ink character recognition*), optical characters (◇ *optical character recognition*) or be *input/output* devices such as *visual display units* and *terminals* able to input by means of *keyboards*, *light pens*, and other means of directly inputting to main memory.

Also known as input unit.

input instruction code An *instruction set* forming part of an automatic language, usually mnemonic, with operations coded to have some appearance of the actual operation (e.g. MPY for multiply, BRN for branch). A type of *pseudo-code* readily understood by the programmer.

input limited Descriptive of a *program* for which the overall processing time is limited by the speed of an *input* unit, so that processing is delayed to await the input of further items for processing. Related to *output limited* and *processor limited*.

input/output (i/o) A medium or device with the function of inserting *data* or *instructions* into a computer and, after processing, transferring such data either to *backing store*, or to another computer system, or to a form suitable for human beings to understand.

input/output buffer An area of *memory* into which data is placed on its way to or from a *peripheral unit*. When a buffer area is used a number of peripheral units can be operated while the *central processor* is processing more data.

input/output interrupt   A momentary pause in processing during which a *central processor* may transmit or receive a unit of data to or from a *peripheral unit*. ◊ *interrupt*.

input/output interrupt indicators   *Indicators* which are set when an *input/output interrupt* occurs.

input/output library   A set of *programs* or *routines* designed to control the operation of *peripheral* devices. Standard routines supplied by computer manufacturers, designed to relieve the programmer of the task of writing routines common to many problems.

input/output limited   Descriptive of a *program* in which the overall processing time is governed by the speed of *input/output peripheral units*; processing is periodically delayed while data is transferred to or from the central processor. Contrasted with *processor limited*.

input/output referencing   The allocation of symbolic names within a *program* to specific *input* or *output devices*, so that the actual device allocated to the program can be determined at *run time*.

input/output register   A *register* which (a) receives *data* from *input devices* and from which data is transferred to the *main memory*, *arithmetic* or *control unit*, and (b) also receives data from these internal units and transfers the data to *output devices*.

input/output routines   Standard *routines* designed to simplify the programming of day-to-day operations involving *input/output* devices.

input/output switching   The allocation of more than one *channel* for communication between *peripheral units* and a *central processor*, allowing connection through any available channel.

input reader   Synonymous with *input routine*.

input register   A *register* which receives data from an *input device* at a comparatively slow speed, holds it only as long as necessary to carry out a transfer at a much higher speed to *main memory*, or to the *arithmetic* or *control unit* register.

input routine   A *routine* which controls and monitors the *reading* of *instructions* and *data* for *input*, either for storage or for immediate use. The routine may be held permanently in *main memory* or may be hard-wired in the processor circuitry.
Also known as input reader.

input section   1. Synonymous with *input routine* in that the section may be a part of a *program* which controls and monitors *input* from an input device to *main memory*. 2. The physical area of a *store* assigned to the reception of input data.

input station   A *terminal* used for *direct data entry*.

input storage   Synonymous with *input area*.

input stream   Control *instructions* and *data* entered from an *input device* under the control of an *input routine*.

input unit   Synonymous with *input device*.

inquiry and transaction processing   Synonymous with *teleprocessing*; *transaction*[2] *processing* from a number of *terminals* which interrogate as well as update.

inquiry character   A transmission control character used to request a response from a connected station. Abbreviated (from enquiry) as ENQ.

inquiry display terminal   Synonymous with *terminal*.

inquiry station   A *terminal* used for interrogating *files* held remotely.

Also known as inquiry unit.

inquiry unit   Synonymous with *inquiry station*.

insert   To *input data* or *instructions* by the use of manually operated switches.

insertion switch   A manually operated switch used to *insert data* or *instructions*.

installation   1. The process of installing a computer, including the preparation of the site and all services required, connection and initial tests, sometimes including *commissioning*. 2. The installed and working computing facility, including remote *terminals*.

installation tape number   A reference number given in an *installation*[2] to a *reel*[3] of *magnetic tape* to identify it. Differentiated from the reference number assigned by the manufacturer of the reel.

instruction   Data which causes a computer to carry out an operation and specifies the values or *locations* of all *operands*. A *program controller* examines each instruction and initiates the specified action. An instruction usually contains an *operator* (indicating the type of command) and one or more *address* parts, and sometimes a *tag*.

Also known as command, order, step.

instruction address   The *address* of a *location* containing an *instruction*.

instruction address register   The *register* which *stores* the *address* of the next *instruction* to be executed, subject to *branches*, *interrupts*, *halts*. The register forms part of the *program controller* and assists the process of retrieving an instruction from *main memory* at the appropriate point in a program sequence.

instruction area   The area of *memory* in which *instructions* are *stored*.
Also known as instruction storage.

instruction character   Synonymous with *control character*.

instruction code   The set of *symbols* and *characters* which constitute
the *instructions* a computer is able to *execute*.
Also known as order code. ⟳ *instruction set* and *machine code*.

instruction constant   A *constant* written in *instruction format* but not
capable of being *executed*; used as a *do-nothing instruction*.

instruction counter   A device which indicates the *location* of the next
instruction in a program sequence. Usually part of, or associated
with, the *program controller*.

instruction deck   Synonymous with *instruction pack*.

instruction, discrimination   Synonymous with *branch instruction*.

instruction format   The specific arrangement of the *digits* which
constitute the various functions of an instruction, including the
operation, the *address* of the next instruction to be carried out, and
addresses of one or more *operands*. Other parts of an instruction
may include a *modifier*, and the addresses of one or more *registers*.
As a minimum an instruction contains digits to represent the function to be carried out and two other groups to represent the addresses
of operands; the format for these in a computer with a twenty-four-
bit word length might be the first four bits for the function code,
the next ten bits for the first operand and the final ten bits for the
second operand. ⟳ *bit-slice microprocessor*.

instruction modification   The process of altering the value of a part
of an *instruction* so that the next time the altered (modified)
instruction is executed it will carry out a different *operation*.
Because an instruction is held as a set of *digits*, the *modification*
process treats the instruction as an item of *data* and carries out an
appropriate *arithmetic* or *logical operation* in order to modify it.

instruction pack   A *pack*[1] of *punched cards* containing *instructions*
for a *program* or *suite*.
Also known as instruction deck.

instruction register   A *register* in the *control unit* in which an
instruction is stored during its execution by the *program controller*.
Also known as control register, program address counter, program
counter, program register.

instruction repertoire   Synonymous with *instruction set*.

instruction set   The *instruction* repertoire available in *machine
code*.

Also known as instruction code, instruction repertoire, machine code, order code.

instruction storage Synonymous with *instruction area*.

instruction time The time required to select and interpret an *instruction*, and step on to the next instruction, but excluding the actual *execution time*.

instruction, waste Synonymous with *do-nothing instruction*.

instruction word A *word* containing an instruction. ⋄ *instruction format*.

integer A whole number; thus a number that does not contain a fractional component. Zero is an integer.

integrated circuit (IC) A complete electronic circuit in which all components, passive and active, are made of a single piece of *semiconductor* material as a result of chemical control (in the manufacturing process) of the purity and courses of the conducting and semiconducting paths. ⋄ *large-scale integration* and *very large-scale integration*.

intelligence Processing capability as contained in an *intelligent terminal*. But *artificial intelligence* is a term reserved for the ability to reason, learn and improve.

intelligent terminal A *terminal* which can not only act as a remote input/output station but can also be *programmed* and provide a local processing capability without having to call on the processing power of the computer to which it is a terminal. A rough indication of intelligence level is provided by the range *dumb terminal* (no intelligence), *smart terminal* (some intelligence), intelligent terminal (rather more than smart) and *front-end processor*.

interactive Synonymous with conversational (⋄ *conversational mode*) implying a dialogue between computer and *terminal* or computer and computer.

interactive mode Synonymous with *conversational mode*.

interblock gap The distance between *blocks* of *records* on *magnetic tape*.

Also known as interrecord gap.

interface 1. A common boundary between systems or devices, represented by the *channels* and associated control circuits making up the connections between a *central processor* and *peripheral units*, or between any two units. 2. A linkage between one *program* and another.

interface routines Linking *routines* between one system and another.

interference The result of unwanted signals in a communications circuit.

interfix A technique used in *information retrieval* systems to describe unambiguously the relation between *keywords* in different *records*, thus ensuring that words which seem related but are not in fact relevant are not retrieved.

interior label A *label* written at the beginning of a *magnetic tape* to identify its contents. Contrasted with *exterior label*, which refers to a written label placed on the outside of a *reel*[3].

interlude A small *routine* which carries out minor preliminary operations usually of a *housekeeping* type, before the main routine is entered. The interlude might, for example, calculate the values of certain parameters.

intermittent error A sporadic *error* which tends to occur before and after any attempt to establish its presence and cause.

internal format The form taken by data and *instructions* when they have been read into *central processor* or *backing store*.

internal fragmentation Disturbance of *main memory* when data is required to fit into less space than is available.

internally stored program A *program* stored in *memory* rather than on a *backing store* or another external medium.

internal memory Synonymous with *main memory*.

internal store Synonymous with *main memory*.

International Algebraic Language An early form of the language which developed into *ALGOL*.

interpreter Synonymous with *interpretive program*.

interpretive code A *pseudo-code* for use with an *interpretive program*.

interpretive program A *program* which translates *pseudo-code instructions* into *machine code* instructions during the operation of the program. The pseudo-instructions are translated by subroutines into machine-code instructions which are then immediately executed.

Also known as interpreter.

interpretive trace program A *trace program* which is also an *interpretive program*. Each *symbolic instruction* is translated into its equivalent *machine code* before it is executed; the result is then recorded.

interrecord gap Synonymous with *interblock gap*.

interrupt 1. A temporary break in the sequence of a *program*, initiated externally and causing control to pass to another *routine*; e.g. a halt generated by a signal from an *input/output* device indicating an operational error. After the disruption, ordinary operation can be resumed from the point of the interrupt. Also known as interruption. 2. To cause such a temporary break.

interruption Synonymous with *interrupt*.

interrupt mask The process of ignoring an *interrupt* and delaying the required action. ⊘ *interrupt stacking*.

interrupt priorities Different types of *interrupt* may be assigned priorities so that if two occur simultaneously the interrupt with the higher priority will be dealt with first.

interrupt signal The *signal* generated to cause an *interrupt*.

interrupt stacking Delaying action on *interrupts* by *interrupt masking*, and, where more than one interrupt occurs during the delay period, forming a queue. Each interrupt is then dealt with in accordance with *interrupt priorities*.

interrupt trap A *switch*[1] which is set under *program* control to prevent or allow an *interrupt*.

intersection Synonymous with *And operation*.

intimate Pertaining to *software* which has a close interaction with *hardware* functions.

Also known as machine-intimate.

inversion Synonymous with *negation*. (But ⊘ *inverted file*.)

inverted file A *file* or form of *file organization* in which an identifying *key* is attached to each characteristic or attribute which may apply to a particular item. For example, if one of the characteristics in a personnel record file is 'job description systems analyst grade 3' this attribute will be followed by the identifying key of all personnel with this attribute. Inverted files are used mainly for *information retrieval*, since they provide rapid satisfaction to inquiries but attract a heavy overhead in *updating*.

inverter A *logical element* with one *binary* input signal, performing the logical function of *negation*.

i/o Abbreviation for *input/output*.

irreversible magnetic process A change of magnetic flux in a magnetic material. The changed condition persists after the magnetic field causing the change has been removed. Contrasted with *reversible magnetic process*.

Also known as irreversible process.

irreversible process Synonymous with *irreversible magnetic process*.

isolated locations *Storage locations* protected by a *hardware* device preventing them from being *addressed* by a user's *program* and protecting their contents from accidental alteration.

item size The number of *characters* or *digits* in a unit of data.

iteration A single cycle of operations in an *iterative routine*.

iterative routine A *routine* which repeatedly performs a series of operations until a specified condition is obtained.

J

jack Synonymous with *socket*.

JCL Abbreviation for *job-control language*.

jitter Brief instability of a signal, applied particularly to signals on a *cathode ray tube*.

job A unit of work organized to be processed by a computer.

job-control language (JCL) A *language* designed to allow communication between user and *operating system*, so that the user can express the appropriate details to ensure that *jobs* are controlled by the operating system.

job-control program A *program* capable of accepting *statements* written in a *job-control language* and interpreting these into *instructions*. These instructions control a *job* run under an *operating system*.

job-flow control Control over the sequence of *jobs* being processed, ensuring the efficient use of *peripheral units* and *central processor*.

join Synonymous with *Or operation*.

joint denial Synonymous with *Nor operation*.

Josephson junction A circuit in which thin film strips are separated by a thin oxide barrier with electrons caused to tunnel across this barrier. Immersion in liquid helium causes the conductivity properties to change, and the circuits switch at very high speeds. ⬦ *junction*.

jump Synonymous with *branch*.

jumper A short length of electrical conductor used temporarily to complete a circuit or to bypass an existing circuit.

jump instruction Synonymous with *branch instruction*.

junction The contact surface between *n-type* and *p-type* semiconducting material, where transistor action occurs.

justify 1. Where necessary, to change the positions of words arranged for printing so that either left-hand or right-hand margins or both are regular. 2. By extension of 1, to move an item in a *register* so that the most or least significant digit is at either the left-hand or right-hand end of the register.

K

k Abbreviation for kilo, used to denote a thousand; also used to denote 'about a thousand' especially when indicating the size of *store*. This presents no problems for a 4k-*word* store, meaning a store with 4096 words; nor is there a problem for 8k-, 16k- or 32k-word stores; but a 64k-word store has 65,536 words, and is therefore sometimes described as a 65k-word store.

Karnaugh map A method of representing in tabular form the relationship between Boolean (◊ *Boolean algebra*) switching functions.

key 1. A digit or group of digits used to identify a *record*. The key may be a code, and is not necessarily a part of the record. 2. A marked button or lever operated manually to generate a *character*.

keyboard A device for generating a *character* by the depression of one of a panel of *keys*.

keypad A hand-held *keyboard*.

keyword The significant or informative word in a phrase, often used as a descriptive word for a document.

kilo- A prefix signifying one thousand. ◊ *k*.

kilomega- A prefix signifying 10^9. Synonymous with *billi-* and *giga-*.

L

label A *character* or group of characters used to identify a *record* or unit of data; usually attached to the data it identifies.
Also known as tab.

label record A *record* identifying a *file* held on a *magnetic memory* medium.

language A defined set of combinations of *characters* or *symbols*, governed by recognized rules. Computers operate *machine code* languages, but can recognize various *high-level languages* through the use of the appropriate *compiler*, which produces *object code* from *source language statements*.

lap To smooth the surface of a *wafer* of *semiconductor* crystal.

large-scale integration (LSI) The process of making *integrated circuits* containing a large number of *logical elements* (perhaps from 100 to 5000) or *memory bits* (perhaps from 1000 to 16,000).
⟡ *very large scale integration*.

laser A device which emits a very narrow beam of electromagnetic energy in the visible light spectrum.

laser emulsion storage A *storage* medium using a controlled *laser* beam to expose areas on a photosensitive surface. The laser beam is interrupted to produce the desired information pattern.

last-in first-out A queuing technique which retrieves from a queue the item most recently placed there.

latch 1. To hold a circuit in position until another operating circuit is ready to change such a circuit. 2. The device which carries out such a process.

latency ⟡ *wait time*.

layout character A *character* which controls the way in which data is to be printed.
Also known as format.

LCD display A *display* using liquid crystal diode technology.

leader A length of paper, blank apart from feed holes, that precedes the data recorded on a reel of *paper tape*.

leading end The end of a piece of *paper tape* on which the first *character* appears.

leaf Last *node* of a *tree*.

leap-frog test A test carried out by a *program* in *memory* which performs tests on data in different *locations*. The program moves from one memory area to another until all locations have been tested.

leased line Synonymous with *private line*.

least significant character The character in the extreme right-hand position of a group of significant *characters* in *positional notation*.

LED Abbreviation for *light-emitting diode*.

LED display A *display* using *light-emitting diodes*.

leg A *path* in a *routine* or *subroutine*.

length The number of *bits* or *characters* forming a *word*, *record* or any other unit of data.

letter A *character* of the alphabet. Contrasted with *symbol* in a *character set*, and hence usually excludes diacritical marks and punctuation marks.

letter out Synonymous with *erase*.

librarian The controller of a *library* of *storage* media and *programs*.

library An organized collection of *programs* or *data files*.

library program A *program* available in or taken from a *program library*.

library routine A *routine* in a *program library*.

library subroutine A *subroutine* in a *program library*.

library tape A *magnetic tape*, usually containing general *routines* used in operating a computer centre, available from a *library*.

library track A *track* used for storing static reference data.

light-emitting diode (LED) A *diode* which emits light when it is excited by an electric current.

light gun Synonymous with *light pen*.

light pen A pen-like high-speed photosensitive device which allows communication between computer user and *terminal*; when the pen is held against the face of the *screen*[1], the point at which it is held can be determined by the computer and as a result other points can be automatically plotted (e.g. lines drawn, rough circles displayed precisely) or selections can be made from a *display menu*.
Also known as light gun.

limiter A device with one input variable and one output variable, used to limit the power of a signal, reducing it when it exceeds a predetermined value.

line 1. A *channel* or conductor able to transmit signals. 2. A horizontal row of *characters* on a page or *terminal screen*. But ▷

hidden line. 3. A *flowline* in a *flowchart*. 4. An *instruction* or *statement* in a *program*, identifed by its *line number*.

linear list Synonymous with *dense list*.

line-at-a-time printer Synonymous with *line printer*.

line driver Synonymous with *bus driver*.

line-feed code A *control character* which specifies the number of lines to be fed through a *line printer* between each line of print.

line, magnetostrictive delay ⇨ *magnetostrictive acoustic delay line*.

line noise *Noise* generated in a *data transmission line*[1].

line number A group of digits identifying an *instruction* or *statement* in a program; *lines*[4] are usually numbered sequentially but not necessarily consecutively.

line printer A high-speed *printer* which prints out results from a computer one line at a time. Contrasted with printers which print a *character* at a time and others which print a page at a time. Also known as line-at-a-time printer.

line, sonic delay Synonymous with *acoustic delay line*.

link A *branch instruction*, or an *address* in such an instruction, used specifically to *exit* from a *subroutine* to pass control or *parameters* to another part of the *program*.
Also known as return address.

linkage editing To carry out the function of *binding* independently *translated programs* and resolving anomalies in cross-references between them.

linkage editor A *program* which carries out the functions of *linkage editing* or *binding*.

linked subroutine Synonymous with *closed subroutine*.

LISP A *high-level language* developed for manipulating symbolic strings in *list processing* and used particularly for text manipulation application. The word is an acronym for LISt Processing.

list 1. To print a series of *records* on a *file* one after another without performing calculations other than to select appropriate records or arrange the records appropriately. ⇨ *list processing*. 2. The printed results of such a process.

list processing Processing data arranged in *list*[2] format, for example, a *chained list* in which the physical location of items remains unaltered while the logical order is changed.

literal operands *Operands*, usually in *source language statements*, which specify the value of a *constant* rather than the *address* in which the constant is stored. The coding is thus more concise than if the constant had been allocated a *data name*.

load 1. To place a *storage* medium into an *input* unit. 2. To cause data or *programs* to be *read* into *memory*.

load-and-go A process in which a *source program* is automatically translated into *machine code* and stored in the *central processor* ready to be performed. There are therefore no delays between *loading* and *execution*.

loader Synonymous with *loading routine*.

loading routine A *routine*, held permanently in *memory*, which enables a *program* to be *loaded*.
Also known as loader, load program.

load program Synonymous with *loading routine*.

local Pertaining to items used only in one defined part of a *program*. Contrasted with *global*.

location Any place in which a unit of data may be *stored*. A location is usually designated by the *address* part of an *instruction word*.

location counter A value, modified (⟡ *modifier*) by *program*, used to *address* a series of *locations*; the modification ensures that a different location is addressed each time the location counter is called.

lock-out 1. To prevent access to, or inhibit the activation of, *hardware* or *software*, especially when such activation would involve an area of memory already being used. 2. A device used to ensure such protection.

log 1. To record events in chronological sequence. 2. A record of a particular series of events, e.g. *operator's log*, *console log*.

logger 1. A device which records a *log*. 2. A device or procedure which allows a user to *log-in*.

logic 1. The science dealing formally with the principles of thought and reasoning. 2. The mathematical treatment of formal logic (⟡ *Boolean algebra*) and its application to the interconnection of circuits.

logical chart Synonymous with *logic flowchart*.

logical comparison The operation performed when two *operands* are examined and a decision taken as to whether they are equal in value or not, and if not, which is greater than the other.

logical decision A yes-or-no choice between alternatives such as two possible paths in a *routine*, the selection being dependent on a negative or positive result to an intermediate problem.

logical diagram ⟡ *logic diagram*.

logical difference The members of one set which are not also members of another set.

logical element The simplest device capable of being represented in a system of symbolic logic; e.g. a *flip-flop*, an *And element*. ◊ *Boolean algebra*.

logical flowchart ◊ *logic flowchart*.

logical instruction Any *instruction* which specifies one of the *logical operations*[1].

logical operation 1. An operation involving the use of *logical operators*, e.g. *And, Nand, Not, Or*, etc. ◊ *Boolean algebra*. 2. A processing operation not involving arithmetic.

logical operator A *word* or symbol representing a logical function which is to be applied to one or more associated *operands*. It may appear in front of the operand (e.g. in the *monadic operation* known as *negation*) but in *dyadic operations* it appears between operands.

logical record A *record* containing all the fields necessary to represent a transaction or to present a specific group of facts.

logical shift A shift operation in which digits are moved from left to right or right to left in such a way that digits moved out of one end of a *word* are brought round to the other end.
Also known as end-around shift.

logical symbol A symbol used to represent one of the *logical operators*.

logical track A group of *tracks* which can be addressed as a single group.

logical unit A group of *characters*, *digits*, or *fields* which represents a transaction or other unit of information.

logic chart Synonymous with *logic flowchart*.

logic diagram A representation of the design of a device or system, in which graphic symbols represent *logical elements* and their relationships.

logic flowchart 1. A chart representing *logical elements* and their relationships. 2. The representation of the logical steps in any *program* by means of a standard set of symbols.

log-in To insert identification data, often to a *terminal*, before starting a dialogue or entering a query.

log-out Synonymous with *log*, but with the implication of *printout* rather than a manual record.

longitudinal-mode delay line A *magnetostrictive delay line* in which the mode of operation depends on longitudinal vibrations in a magnetostrictive material.

longitudinal redundancy check (LRC) An error detection process performed on a group of *characters* or *bits* rather than on each character or bit. The group is seen as a longitudinal formation.

look ahead The process of *masking* and *interrupt* until the following *instruction* has been executed.

look-up To select a data item, identified by a *key*, from a *table*.

look-up table A data *list* so arranged that a *look-up* process can retrieve data identified by specified *keys*.

loop A closed sequence of *instructions* performed repeatedly until a test shows that a specified condition is satisfied, at which point a *branch instruction* is obeyed and the program *exits* from the loop.

loop body The main part of a *loop*, undertaking the primary purpose of the loop rather than handling the tests and exit.

loop testing Those *instructions* in a *loop*, outside the *loop body*, which establish whether the objectives of the loop have been achieved, e.g. that the loop has been carried out a specified number of times.

loss Synonymous with *attenuation*.

low-level language A programming language close to *machine code* and in which each *instruction* has a one-for-one equivalent in machine code.

low order The significance given to certain *characters* or *digits* farthest to the right in a number.

low-order position The right-hand or least-significant position of a number or *word*.

LPM Abbreviation for lines per minute.

LRC Abbreviation for *longitudinal redundancy check*.

LSI Abbreviation for *large-scale integration*.

machine address Synonymous with *absolute address*.

machine code An *operation code* which can be recognized by a machine, and which represents the *instruction repertoire* of a computer.
Also known as computer code, instruction set, machine instruction code, machine language code.

machine error An *error* caused by a machine malfunction rather than by a *software* or operating fault.

machine independent Pertaining to a *program* or procedure prepared without consideration of a specific *machine code*.

machine-independent language A *programming language* designed to be capable of being interpreted by any computer equipped with an appropriate *compiler*. Most *high-level languages* are in theory machine-independent, but computer manufacturers accentuate certain language features which may set the *architecture* of their own machine to particular advantage, and this limits the *portability* of programs written in machine-independent languages.

machine instruction An *instruction* written directly in *machine code* and not requiring translation.

machine instruction code Synonymous with *machine code*.

machine-intimate Synonymous with *intimate*.

machine language *Instructions* written in *machine code*.

machine language code Synonymous with *machine code*.

machine-readable Capable of being *read* by an *input device*.

macro A set of *instructions* or *statements* which can be activated by use of the name given to the set. ⋄ *macroassembler*, *macro-instruction*.
Also known as macrocode.

macroassembler An *assembler* which recognizes *macros* and generates *machine code* instructions. A macroassembler may also allow segmentation of a *program* for testing, as well as the provision of facilities for program analysis in the *debugging* process.
Also known as macroassembly program.

macroassembly program Synonymous with *macroassembler*.

macrocode Synonymous with *macroinstruction*.

macroelement Synonymous with *data element chain*.

macro flowchart A table or chart used in the design of the logic of a *routine*; the various segments and *subroutines* of the routine are represented by *blocks*. The detailed design of the routine is not considered in the macro flowchart.

macrogenerator A *program* with the function of replacing *source language macros* with sets of *instructions* in the same source language.

macroinstruction A single *instruction* which generates a number of *machine code* instructions; these are a cluster of instructions for carrying out a commonly used function, perhaps more variable than a *subroutine*.

macroprogramming The use of *macros* in preparing a *program*.

magnetic disk A *storage device* consisting of a number of flat circular magnetically coated plates, on the surface of which data is stored in the form of magnetic spots arranged as *binary* data. The plates or disks are coated on each side, and each surface has a number of *tracks* for data, which is read from or written to the tracks by *read/write heads*. ⊘ *floppy disk*.

magnetic disk file A *file* of data held on a *magnetic disk*.

magnetic disk store ⊘ *magnetic disk*.

magnetic drum A *storage* device consisting of a cylinder coated with magnetizable material; the cylinder rotates past a set of *read/write heads* which coincide with recording *tracks* on the surface of the cylinder. *Binary coded* data is recorded serially as the drum rotates, and data can be read from or written to any of the tracks.

magnetic film ⊘ *thin film* memory.

magnetic head A small electromagnet, usually horseshoe-shaped, used to read, record or erase polarized spots on a magnetic medium.

magnetic ink character recognition (MICR) The automatic recognition of characters recorded on documents by means of ink containing particles of magnetizable material.

magnetic memory A *storage* device which operates using a film of magnetic material for registering or recovering information in the form of *bits*.

Also known as magnetic store.

magnetic mirror A device based on the principle that ions in a magnetic field tend to be reflected away from magnetic fields which are higher than average.

magnetic store   Synonymous with *magnetic memory*.

magnetic tape   A tape, usually oxide-coated polyester film, on which data can be stored as a series of magnetized spots.

magnetic tape deck   Synonymous with *tape deck*.

magnetic tape drive   Synonymous with *tape deck*.

magnetic tape file   A reel of *magnetic tape* containing *records* arranged in an ordered sequence.

magnetic tape unit   Synonymous with *tape deck*.

magnetostriction   A property of certain materials which causes them to change in length when they are magnetized.

magnetostrictive acoustic delay line   An *acoustic delay line* in which the effects of *magnetostriction* convert electrical signals to sonic waves, and vice versa.

magnitude   Of a number or quantity, the absolute value irrespective of its sign; e.g. the magnitude of -5 is 5.

mail box   An area of *memory* reserved for data addressed to certain *peripheral units*, including other processors.

main frame   The sense of this phrase has moved swiftly: first it referred to the framework of a computer which contained the *arithmetic and logic unit*; then it was used to refer to the *central processor* itself; and now tends to be used to refer to large computers, distinguishing them from *microcomputers, microprocessors* and *minicomputers*.

main memory   Internal *memory* – the immediate access store as opposed to *backing store*.
Also known as internal memory, internal store.

maintenance routine   A *routine* designed to help a service engineer carry out routine preventative maintenance.

majority   A *logical operator* with the property that if p is a statement, q is a statement, r is a statement, . . ., then the majority of p.q.r. . . ., is true if more than half the statements are true, false if half or less than half are true.

majority carrier   The predominant carrier in a semiconductor; in an *n-type* semiconductor, which has more electrons than holes, electrons are the majority carrier; in a *p-type* semiconductor holes outnumber electrons and are the majority carrier.

malfunction routine   A *routine* designed to trace a *hardware* fault or to help in diagnosing an error in a *program*.

mantissa The fractional part of a logarithm; the mantissa is always positive.

manual input Entering data by hand (e.g. by *keyboard* operation), usually during processing.

manual operation Using manual methods to process data, for example by setting a succession of manual switches.

manual word generator A unit which allows a *word* to be entered directly into *memory* as a result of a *manual operation*.

map 1. A list produced by a *compiler*; the list helps a programmer relate *data names* to specific *addresses*. 2. Means of transforming *virtual addresses* into *absolute addresses*.

marginal test A test carried out to establish whether a piece of equipment can operate within predetermined operating tolerances.

Markov chain A model for a sequence of events in which the probability of one event is dependent only on the state of the preceding event.

mask A pattern of *characters* or *bits* used to specify which parts of another *bit pattern* or *word* are to be operated on.
Also known as filter.

mask bit A *bit* used to extract a selected bit from a *string*.

masking A technique of using a *mask* to operate on a *bit pattern* to select certain processes and ignore others.

mask register A *register* used for *masking*.

mass storage A *backing store* of large capacity, usually directly *on-line* to a *central processor*, e.g. *magnetic disk*, *magnetic drum*.
Also known as bulk storage, although this phrase is also used for any form of backing store.

master clock A device capable of generating clocking pulses to maintain the time frequency of the circuits.

master control program A *program* which controls the operation of a system, either in the sense of linking *subroutines* and calling *segments* into memory as required, or as a program controlling *hardware* and limiting the amount of intervention required by a human operator.

master file A main *file* of reference data which is relatively permanent and provides routine data, updated periodically by data which is relatively less permanent.

master library tape A reel of *magnetic tape* which contains all the *programs* and major *subroutines* required in a data processing installation.
Also known as master program file.

master program file Synonymous with *master library tape*.

master record A *record* in a *file*; a master record is *updated* by a *change record*.

master/slave system A system in which a central computer has control over, and is connected to, one or more *satellite computers*.

match 1. Synonymous with *equivalence* operation. 2. To compare the *keys* of two *records* in order to select one for a further stage of processing or to reject an invalid (i.e. non-matching) record.

material implication Synonymous with *conditional implication operation*.

meet Synonymous with *And operation*.

mega- A prefix signifying a million, e.g. as in megabit, meaning one million *bits*.

memory Synonymous with *main memory*. But sometimes *backing store* devices are referred to as memory units.

memory capacity The number of units of data that can be stored in *memory*, expressed as the number of *locations* available.

memory cycle The sequence of operations required to insert or extract a unit of data from *memory*.

memory dump To output the contents of some or all *locations* in *memory* either during *program testing*, during an attempt to diagnose a *software error*, or at regular *checkpoints* as a precaution against *hardware* or *software* malfunction. Contents are dumped either as a *printout* or to a *backing store*.

memory fill The placing of predetermined patterns of characters in *memory registers* not in use in a particular *program*; if an error causes the program to *address* these registers then the *error* condition is signalled by the predetermined pattern.

memory guard A *hardware* or *software* device which ensures that a *program* cannot *address* specified *locations* in *memory*.

memory protect A *hardware* device which protects each *program*, and its data, in a *multiprogramming* environment, from being mutilated by another program.

memory, random-access ◊ *random-access memory*.

menu ◊ *display menu*.

mercury delay line An *acoustic delay line* in which mercury recirculates sonic signals.
Also known as Hg delay line.

merge An operation performed on two, or more, ordered sets of *records* to create a single set or *file*.
Also known as collate.

message A combination of *characters* and symbols designed to communicate *information*.

message display console A console unit incorporating a *cathode ray tube* and allowing *messages* to be displayed. Data stored in *memory* can be displayed as a page.

message queuing In a *data communications* system, a technique for controlling the handling of messages, allowing them to be accepted by a computer and stored until they have been processed or routed to another destination.

message switching system A *data communications* system in which a central computer services several distant *terminals*, receiving *messages* and storing them until they can be retransmitted to another destination.

metacompilation The process of using *compilers* to compile other compilers used to compile *programs* for *execution*.

MICR Abbreviation for *magnetic ink character recognition*.

micro- 1. A prefix denoting one millionth (10^{-6}) as in microsecond, one millionth of a second. 2. More commonly, a prefix denoting small, as in *microinstruction, microprocessor*.

microcircuit A miniaturized electronic circuit consisting of elements which are interconnected and so manufactured that they are inseparable.

microcircuit isolation The electrical insulation of circuit elements from the conducting silicon *wafer* in the manufacturing process of a *microcircuit*.

Microcobol A *high-level language* developed by Computer Analysts and Programmers for business-orientated microprocessor programming. Related to *COBOL*.

microcode Synonymous with *microinstruction*.

microcoding In *programming*, the use of certain operations not ordinarily accessible, such as parts of the *arithmetic operations*. A series of such steps might be used to form a *macroinstruction* such as square root. ⇔ *microprogram*.

microcomputer A *microprocessor* with *peripheral unit interfaces*, allowing a complete computing system. A *central processor* may be on a single microprocessor chip, and the system may also have *ROM storage*, *clock* circuits and *input/output interfaces*, *selector registers* and *control circuits*.

microelectronics The use of solid circuits in which units of *semiconductors* are formed into a number of components.

micro flowchart A *flowchart* showing detailed *program* steps, from which *coding* can be carried out. ⇔ *block flowchart*.

microinstruction A small, single basic *instruction* representing a simple concept such as add, compare or delete. Used in *microcoding*. ⇔ *microprogram*.
Also known as microcode.

microminiaturization The reduction in size and increase in *packing density* of electronic components and circuit elements, resulting in less space, less power and less delay in signal propagation.

microprocessor Commonly used as a synonym for *microcomputer*, implying *central processor* and *peripheral unit interfaces*. Originally, confined to the central processor and implying that all elements are contained on a single *chip*.

microprogram A *program* written in *microinstructions*, defining a specific *hardware* function. The microprogram addresses the *control unit* directly and is not accessible to the user. *Bit-slice microprocessors* are, however, microprogrammable.

middleware System *software* tailored to a particular user's needs.

milli- A prefix meaning one thousandth (10^{-3}), as in millisecond.

minicomputer A computer which does not require the closely controlled *environment*[1] of *main frame* computers, and has a richer *instruction set* than that of a *microprocessor*.

minimal tree A *tree* whose terminal *nodes* have been so ordered that the tree operates at optimum effectiveness.

minimum access code A coding system which minimizes the time needed to retrieve a unit of data from a *storage device*.
Also known as a minimum delay code, minimum latency code, optimum code.

minimum delay code Synonymous with *minimum access code*.

minimum latency code Synonymous with *minimum access code*.

minority carrier The non-dominant carrier in a *semiconductor*. ⇔ *majority carrier*.

minuend One of the *operands* used in subtraction; the quantity from which another quantity, the *subtrahend*, is subtracted.

minus zone The *character* or *digit position* which displays the algebraic sign of an *operand*.

mixed base notation The representation of numbers or quantities where any two or more adjacent digit positions have a different *radix notation*.
Also known as mixed radix notation.

mixed radix notation ⇔ *mixed base notation*.

MNOS Abbreviation for metal nitride silicon device.

mobility The drift of ions (e.g. electrons and holes in *semiconductors*) under applied electric fields; the intrinsic current-carrying property of n- and p-*doped* silicon.

mode A method of operation.

modem Acronym for modulator/demodulator. A device which allows data to be transmitted over telephone circuits.

modification The process of changing the *address* part of an *instruction* as a result of *executing* previous instructions in a *program*. ◊ *modifier*.

modifier A *word* or quantity used to alter an *instruction* to cause the *execution* of an instruction different from the original one. As a result, the same instruction, successively altered by a modifier, may be used repetitively to carry out a different operation each time it is used. ◊ *modify*.

modify To change the *address* part of an *instruction* so that there is a different *operand* each time the routine containing the instruction is performed. ◊ *program modification*.

modulate To carry out *modulation*.

modulation The process of adjusting signals to a required standard, as in the conversion of signals emitted by an output device to a standard required for transmission on a telephone circuit.

modulator A device which superimposes a data signal on a carrier wave.

modulator/demodulator ◊ *modem*.

module A part of a *program* which performs a specific function and can be tested on its own.

modulo A mathematical operation in which the result is the remainder after a specified number has been divided; e.g. 29 modulo 4 = 1.

monadic operation A processing operation performed on one *operand*.

monitor *Hardware* or *software* which examines the status of a system to identify any deviation from prescribed operational conditions.

monolithic Relating to the single silicon *substrate* in which an *integrated circuit* is constructed.

morpheme A linguistic unit which indicates relationships between words or ideas; a conjunction such as and, with, not.

MOS Acronym for metal oxide semiconductor.

most significant character The character at the extreme left-hand position of a group of significant characters in *positional nota-tion*.

mother board A rigid frame to which *circuit boards* are attached to form the basis of a *microprocessor*.

Also known as back plane, chassis.

MPU Abbreviation for *microprocessor* unit.

multi-access system A system which allows a number of people to *access* a *central processor* in *conventional mode* virtually simultaneously.

multi-address instruction An *instruction* which specifies the address of more than one *operand*.

multichip A circuit consisting of two or more *semiconductor wafers*, each containing a single element.

multi-level addressing Synonymous with *indirect addressing*.

multilinked list A *list* in which each item has at least two *pointers*.

multiple-length number An *operand* which exceeds the capacity of one *word*.

multiple-length working A method of carrying out operations on data in such a way that two or more *words* are used to represent data items, usually to achieve greater *precision*.

multiplex To arrange a transmission facility so that two or more messages can be transmitted simultaneously.

multiplexed operation A system in which a number of simultaneous operations share a common unit in such a way that each appears to be an independent operation.

multiplexer ◊ *multiplexor*.

multiplexor A device capable of interleaving two or more streams of events or of distributing such interleaved events to the appropriate systems. This allows a *central processor* to be connected to a number of *communication channels* to receive or transmit data.

Also known as multiplexer.

multiplexor channel A *channel* able to accept the interleaving of many simultaneous transmissions in both directions.

multiplicand One of the factors used in *multiplication*; a quantity which is multiplied by another, called the *multiplier^2*.

Also known as icand.

multiplication The arithmetic process in which a result (the *product*) is obtained from two factors, the *multiplicand* and the *multiplier^2*.

multiplication time The time required to multiply two specified *operands*.

multiplier 1. A device which generates a *product* by additions of the *multiplicand* in accordance with the value of the multiplier[2]. 2. One of the factors used in multiplication; that number which is used to multiply another, the *multiplicand*.
Also known as ier.

multi-precision arithmetic The use of two or more *words* for multiple-length working, particularly where undesired inaccuracy would have resulted if only a single word had been used.

multiprocessing The use of a number of independently usable *central processors*, each of which has access to a common jointly addressable *memory*. Each processor is capable of processing the same applications as those being processed by the other processors, thus providing extra *resilience* to the total system. Contrasted with *multiprogramming*, in which a single processor operates a number of *programs* independently. Under multiprocessing, several processors can share a program simultaneously.

multiprocessor A *central processor* with two or more *arithmetic and logic units* that can be used simultaneously.

multiprocessor interleaving The allocation of *memory* areas to the different processors of a *multiprocessing* system to avoid interaction between *programs* being run simultaneously.

multiprogramming The interleaved execution of two or more *programs*, so that it appears that the programs are being executed at the same time. This allows part of one program to be executed while another waits for completion of, for example, a slow *input/output* operation, and results in improved utilization of the system.
Also known as multirunning.

multirunning Synonymous with *multiprogramming*.

multistation Descriptive of a *communications network* with several *data terminals*.

multitasking The concurrent execution of two or more tasks, usually under *program* control. Common *routines*, *memory* areas and *backing store* are used.

multithread The design of a *program* so that it has more than one logical path through it, each being executed concurrently.

N

NAK Negative acknowledgement, a signal sent by a receiver as a negative response to a sender, indicating that the previous *block* was unacceptable.

Nand Synonymous with *Not-And*.

nano- Prefix denoting one thousand millionth (10^{-9}), as in nanosecond, one thousand millionth of a second.

nano processor A processor operating in the nanosecond cycle range. ⟡ *nano-*.

narrative Explanatory text added to *program instructions*.
Also known as comment.

narrow band A communication line similar to the voice grade line but operating on a lower frequency.

natural-function generator A unit which accepts one or more *input variables* and provides an *output variable* based on a mathematical function.

negation An operation carried out on a single *operand* producing a result in which the significance of each digit position is reversed.
Also known as inversion.

negative feedback The process of returning part of the output to the input in such a way that increased output results in the deduction of a greater quantity from the input.

negator An element which accepts one *binary* input signal and which has the ability to provide a single binary output signal of the opposite significance.
Also known as Not element.

Neither-Nor operation Synonymous with *Nor operation*.

nesting A *program* design technique in which a *routine* or *subroutine* contains a structure similar to itself. In this way, a *loop* may contain another loop and that loop may contain yet another.

network Any system consisting of interconnecting components, with the implication that telecommunications devices are used for the transmission of data between the components.

network constant One of the resistance, inductance, mutual-inductance or capacitance values in a network.

nexus A point in a system at which interconnections occur.

nibble   A four-*bit word*.

nickel delay line   A *delay line* which utilizes the magnetic and *magnetostrictive* properties of nickel to impart delay in a pulse.

nil pointer   A *pointer* which indicates the end of a *chained list*.

NMOS   Metal oxide *semiconductor* circuits using currents of negative charges (and thus faster than *PMOS* circuits made up of positive charges).

n-n junction   A junction between *n-type semiconductors* with different electrical properties.

no-address instruction   An *instruction* in which it is not necessary to specify an *address* in *memory*.

node   An atom or component in a *network*; an element in a *tree*.

noise   A signal with no function, usually caused by a disturbance such as an unplanned variation in voltage. Spurious signals generated by such a disturbance can introduce errors.

noise level   The strength of *noise* in a circuit.

noisy mode   A method of *floating-point arithmetic* associated with normalization, in which *digits* other than zero are introduced in low-order positions during a left shift. These digits appear to be *noise*, although they have in fact been deliberately introduced.

non-arithmetic shift   Synonymous with *logical shift*.

non-destructive read   The reading of data from *memory* in such a way that the data is retained in the source *location*.

non-equivalence operation   Synonymous with *Exclusive-Or* operation.

non-volatile memory   A *storage* medium which continues to hold data after power has been disconnected. A *programmable read-only memory*, once *programmed*, is non-volatile, while a basic *random-access memory* has a volatile memory.

Input		Output
p	q	r
1	0	0
1	1	0
0	1	0
0	0	1

Rules for Nor element

no-operation instruction   Synonymous with *do-nothing instruction*.

Nor element   A *logical element* operating with *binary digits* which provides an output signal in accordance with the rules given in the table on page 128.

Also known as Nor gate.

Nor gate   Synonymous with *Nor element*.

normal contact   A contact which in its normal position closes a circuit and allows current to flow.

normalize   In programming using *floating-point numbers* – to adjust the *fixed-point part* of a number so that the fixed-point part is within a predetermined range.

Nor operation   A logical operation applied to two *operands*. A result is produced depending on the *bit* pattern of the operands and according to the following rules for each binary digit position:

Operands		Result
p	q	r
1	0	0
0	1	0
1	1	0
0	0	1

Also known as dagger operation.

Not-And   A *logical operator* having the property that if p is a statement, q is a statement and r is a statement, then p.q.r. . . . is true if at least one statement is false; and p.q.r. . . . is false if all the statements are true.

Also known as Nand, Not-Both.

Not-And operation   A *logical operation* applied to at least two *operands* which produces a result according to the *bit* patterns of the operands as follows:

Operands		Result
p	q	r
0	1	1
1	0	1
1	1	0
0	0	1

Also known as alternative denial, dispersion.

notation   A systematic method of representing data through the use of characters and symbols; commonly applied to *number systems* using *positional notation*.

Not-Both   Synonymous with *Not-And*.

Not circuit   A circuit which provides an output signal of reverse phase or polarity from the input signal.

Not element   Synonymous with *negator*.

noughts complement   The *radix* complement of a number, obtained by subtracting each digit of the number from one less than its *radix* and then adding 1 to the result thus obtained.

nought state   Synonymous with *zero condition*.

n-plus-one address instruction   An *instruction* formed of a number of *addresses* plus one particular address specifying the *location* of the next instruction.

n-p-n transistor   A junction transistor with a *p-type* slice between two slices of *n-type semiconductor*.

n-type   *Semiconductor* crystal material which has been *doped* with minute quantities of an impurity to produce donor centres of electrons. Because the electrons are negative particles, the material is known as n-type, and the electron conduction (negative) exceeds the hole conduction (absence of electrons). Contrasted with *p-type*.

null instruction   Synonymous with *do-nothing instruction*.

null string   A *string*[2] with no *characters*.

Also known as empty string.

number system   Any system for representing numeric values or quantities.

numeral   One of a set of digits that may be used in a particular *number system*.

numeric   Pertaining to numbers. Contrasted with *alphabetic*.

numeric character   A *character* used as a digit in a *number system*; e.g. in *decimal notation* one of the characters 0 to 9.

numeric code   The representation of data as coded groups of *bits* to denote numerals. Contrasted with *alphabetic code*.

numeric data   Any *field* of *characters* which contains *numeric characters* only.

numeric string   A *string* in which the *characters* are *numeric characters*.

O

object code   The *instructions* of an *object program*.

object computer   The computer for which an *object program* has been prepared. (A different type of computer may be used to *compile* the program.)

object deck   Synonymous with *object pack*.

object language   The set of *instructions* into which a *compiler* translates a *source language*; usually a *machine code* language directly intelligible to a processor. ⟐ *object program*.
Also known as catalanguage, target language.

object pack   The *punched cards* in which an *object program* is held.
Also known as object deck.

object program   A *program* in *object language* produced by translating (by means of a *compiler*) a program written in a *source language*. The object program is usually in a *machine code* capable of being directly intelligible to a computer (although some *high-level languages* produce an object program which may itself need further translation before it is reduced to machine code).
Also known as target program.

OCR   Abbreviation for *optical character recognition*.

octal   A *number system* using eight as a base or *radix*. The octal system uses the digits 0, 1, 2, 3, 4, 5, 6, 7, and each digit position represents a power of eight. Octal notation is sometimes used as a way of representing a *string* of *bits*, e.g. the string 010000101 is considered as three *binary coded* octal numbers 010 000 101, i.e. 205. Thus the string 010000101 can be represented as 'octal' 205, or # 205. *Hexadecimal* is a more usual number system for microprocessor users.

octet   An eight-*bit byte*.

odd-even check   Synonymous with *parity check*.

odd parity check   A *parity check* in which the number of 1 *bits* (as opposed to 0 bits) in a group is expected to be odd. Contrasted with *even parity check*.

off-line   Not under the control of a *central processor*, but relevant to the successful operation of a system; e.g. the transcription of data from *punched cards* to *magnetic tape*. Contrasted with *on-line*.

one-address instruction   An *instruction format* which describes one *address part* involving one *storage location* only.

one-digit adder   Synonymous with *half adder*.

one element   Synonymous with *Or element*.

one gate   Synonymous with *Or element*.

one-level address   Synonymous with *absolute address*.

one-level code   Synonymous with *absolute code*.

one-level store   A method of treating all *on-line storage*, whatever its physical characteristics, as being of one directly accessible *memory*.

one-level subroutine   A *subroutine* which does not itself call a lower level of subroutine during its operation.

one-plus-one address   The *address format* for a system in which each *instruction* contains provision for specifying one operation and two addresses, one showing the *location* of the data to be operated on and the second showing the location of the next instruction to be performed.

one-shot circuit   Synonymous with *single-shot circuit*.

one-step operation   Manual operation of a *central processor*, in which a single *instruction* is carried out in response to a manual control, allowing detailed error diagnosis.

on-line   Under the control of a *central processor*; equipment or systems in interactive communication as well as *terminal* equipment connected to a transmission line. Contrasted with *off-line*.

onomasticon   A list of proper nouns used as a *look-up table* to expand titles, etc., from *keywords*.

op code   Abbreviation for *operation code*.

open code   *Instructions* which must still be written after *macroinstructions* have been used for major steps in a *program*.

open-ended program   A *program* designed so that it can be extended without the need for alteration.

open routine   A *routine* capable of being directly inserted into a larger routine without the need for a *link* or *calling sequence*. Also known as direct-insert routine.

open shop   The organization of a data processing *installation*[2] so that programmers have access to the machine room. Contrasted with a *closed shop* in which only specialist operations staff have access. Also known as hands-on operation.

open subroutine   A *subroutine* which must be inserted directly into a main *routine* each time it is used, without requiring merely a *calling sequence*. Contrasted with *closed subroutine*.

operand The item in an *operation*[1] from which the *result* is obtained as a result of defined actions.

operating ratio The ratio of the number of effective hours of computer operations to the total number of hours of scheduled operation.

operating system The basic *software* or *firmware* which supervises and controls the running of other (user-orientated) *programs*; the operating system allows the system to operate the user programs, controlling the input and output functions and passing control from one program to the next in *multiprogramming*.

operation 1. The means by which a *result* is obtained from an *operand*. 2. An action defined by a single *instruction*. 3. An action defined by a single *logical element*.

operational amplifier Synonymous with *computing amplifier*.

operation code The *code* specifying which *operation* is to be performed.
Also known as op code.

operation cycle That part of a machine cycle during which the actual execution of an *instruction* takes place.

operation decoder A circuit capable of interpreting the *operation* part of an *instruction* and switching to the circuits required for the execution of that instruction.

operation part That part of an *instruction* in which is specified the *operation* to be performed; contains the *operation code*.

operation register A *register* in which the *operation code* is stored during an *operation cycle*.

operation time The time required for an *operation* to complete the *operation cycle*.

operator 1. A person who operates a machine. 2. In an *operation*[1], the element which defines what action is to be performed on the *operand*. 3. A *character* or symbol which designates an operation, e.g. +, −, etc.

optical character recognition (OCR) The identification of printed graphic characters by means of photosensitive devices.

optimal merge tree A *tree* so ordered that *strings* are *merged* with the fewest possible number of *operations*.

optimum code Synonymous with *minimum access code*.

optional halt instruction An *instruction* which will cause a *central* *processor* to halt a *program* under predetermined conditions.

Also known as optional stop instruction.

optional stop instruction Synonymous with *optional halt instruction*.

Oracle A broadcast television text message service similar to *Ceefax*.

Or circuit Synonymous with *Or element*.

order Synonymous with *instruction*.

order code Synonymous with *instruction code*.

orderly close-down The unplanned stopping of a system in such a way that no messages or data are lost or mutilated and a successful re-start is possible when the cause of the stoppage has been obviated.

Or element A *logical element* operating with *binary digits*, and providing an output signal from two input signals, according to the following rules:

Input		Output
p	q	r
1	0	1
1	1	1
0	1	1
0	0	0

Also known as one gate, one element, Or circuit, Or gate.

Or gate Synonymous with *Or element*.

origin The *absolute address* of the start of a *program* or a *block* of coding or an item in *memory* to which reference is made by *relative* or *indirect addressing*.

Also known as float factor.

Or operation A *logical operation* applied to two *operands*. A result is produced depending on the *bit* pattern of the operands and according to the following rules for each binary digit position:

Operands		Result
p	q	r
1	0	1
1	1	1
0	1	1
0	0	0

Also known as Inclusive-Or, disjunction, Either-Or.

oscillating sort   An external *magnetic tape sort* which utilizes the ability of magnetic tape to be moved in either direction.

out connector   On a *flowchart*, a *connector* symbol indicating that the flowline is continued at another place.

out-of-line coding   *Instructions* in a *routine* stored in a different part of the *program storage* from the main routine; possibly added later as a *patch*[2].

output   1. Information and data transferred from *memory* to devices such as *printers* or *terminal screens* or to *backing store*; results produced by such a process. 2. To transfer information and data from memory to such devices.

output area   Synonymous with *output block*.

output block   A part of *memory* reserved for *output* data, from which it is transferred to an output device.
Also known as output area.

output device   Any device capable of receiving information from a *central processor*. An output device may be a *backing store* unit, or a *peripheral unit* which transcribes information on to another medium, e.g. a *printer*, *paper tape punch*, *visual display unit*.

output limited   Description of a *program* for which the overall processing time is limited by the speed of an *output* unit, so that further processing is delayed while output takes place. Related to *input limited* and *processor limited*.

output program   A *program* designed to cause the transcription of data to an *output device*.

output punch   1. An *output device* which transcribes information on to *punched paper tape*. 2. An output device which transcribes information on to *punched cards*.

output routine A *routine* which carries out the processing necessary for the transcription of data to an *output device.*

output routine generator A *generator* which produces an *output routine* in accordance with given specifications.

overflow The generation, as a *result* of an *arithmetic operation*, of a quantity which is beyond the capacity of the result *location*. Contrasted with *underflow.*

overflow indicator An *indicator* set when *overflow* occurs in the *register* with which it is associated.

overlay A *programming* technique used during the operation of a long *program* to allow the same area of *memory* to be used repeatedly for different parts of the program. Each part of the program that is to share the same overlay area is held on *backing store* and read into the area by means of a *control program*, so that by the time the program has been executed several *routines* may have occupied the same group of storage locations at different times.

overlay tree A diagrammatic representation showing the relationships of different *segments* of an *overlay program*[1], indicating how the segments will use the same *memory* area at different times.

overrun The condition which occurs when data is transferred to or from a non-buffered (◊ *buffer*) *control unit* with a *synchronous* medium and the activity initiated by *program* exceeds the *channel* capacity.

overwrite To place data in a *location*, and destroy or mutilate the data previously contained in that location.

own coding The addition to a standard *routine* of user-written *coding* in order to extend its capabilities or reflect special circumstances in the user's environment.

P

pack 1. A set of *punched cards*. 2. To compress data and by so doing conserve space in a *storage* medium. 3. An assembly of *magnetic disks*.

package 1. The plastic, ceramic or metal in which a finished *chip* is mounted. 2. A generalized *program* written to cover the possible requirements of many users. A package is likely to be less efficient than a purpose-built program designed to suit the special requirements of one user, but will have the compensating advantages of immediate availability and less cost.

packet A set of *bits* capable of being transmitted in a data transmission network as a single unit. In a *packet switching* system the packet is likely to include *control* bits and *error* control bits as well as data bits.

packet switching Data transmission storing and forwarding *messages* as addressed *packets* very rapidly from *node* to node in a *network*. The *channel* is occupied only during the short time a packet is transmitted.

packing density The number of units of information for each unit length of a given recording surface.

Also known as data density.

PAD *Packet* assembler and disassembler.

pad ◊ *keypad*.

pad character A *character* used to fill a blank to make up a *record* or *block* to a fixed size. ◊ *padding*.

padding The filling out of a *block* or *record* with blank *characters*, *words* or records to make it up to some fixed size.

page 1. A *block* of fixed length, or a fixed number of blocks, which can be located as one entity in *storage*. 2. Data arranged to form a *screen* on a *terminal*.

paging The procedure of transferring *pages*[1] of data between *main memory* and *backing store*.

paper tape A *storage* medium which consists of a long strip of paper into which holes are punched in a row across the width of the tape, different patterns of holes signifying different *characters*.

paper tape reader A device which recognizes data punched as holes in *paper tape* and transmits it as machine-recognizable signals to a *central processor*.

paper throw   Movement of paper through a *printer* to a specified position other than the next standard printing position.

parallel processing   The processing of all elements of an item of information simultaneously. Contrasted with *serial*.

parallel search storage   Synonymous with *associative storage*.

parallel transmission   The transmission of all *bits* of a *character* at the same time.

parameter   A quantity which may be given variable values.

parameter card   A *punched card* that contains input data which represents special *instructions* for the specific application of a general routine.
Also known as control card.

parasitic signal   An unwanted high-frequency or low-frequency signal in an electronic circuit.

parity bit   A *bit* added to an *array* of bits to make the sum of all the bits (including the parity bit) odd (odd parity) or even (even parity) and thus provide a check that data has been accurately transmitted.

parity check   A check carried out before or after the transfer of data to ensure that the *parity bit* is appropriate to the data transferred.
Also known as odd-even check.

PASCAL   A *high-level language*.

pass   1. The movement of a complete *magnetic tape* past the *read/write heads* in processing a *file*. 2. A single *execution* of a *loop*.

password   A message used in a specified way to identify a user's right to gain access to protected *files* or devices.

patch   1. To change a *routine* by adding a set of *instructions* in *out-of-line coding* and causing these to be entered by means of a *transfer instruction*. 2. The set of instructions formed by such a patching process.

path   A sequence of *instructions* in a *program*; there may be many possible paths in one program.

PC board   Abbreviation for *printed circuit board*.

PCM   Abbreviation for *pulse code modulation*.

pel   A picture element of a *terminal screen*.
Also known as pixel.

peripheral   Used as a synonym for *peripheral unit*.

peripheral interface channel   ⟡ *interface*.

peripheral limited   A system condition which occurs when the time taken to complete a process is dictated by the time taken by *peripheral units* rather than the time taken by the *central processor*. Contrasted with *processor limited*.

peripheral transfer   The transfer of data between a *central processor* and a *peripheral unit*, or between peripheral units.

peripheral unit   Any device capable of being operated under control of a *central processor*, but distinguished from equipment whose control is the sole purpose of a processor. For example, *magnetic disks* and *terminals* are regarded as peripheral units, while numerical control tools are not.

PERT   Acronym for Program Evaluation and Review Technique – a *critical path method*.

phantom circuit   A superimposed circuit resulting from the wires of a pair of circuits being arranged in parallel.

phase jitter   An unwanted random signal distortion.

philoxenic   Friendly to uninformed users, as in *viewdata* systems.

phosphor dots   Elements of a *cathode ray tube* which glow red, green or blue.

phosphorescence   The phenomenon of emitting light for a period after removal of a source of excitation; a *cathode ray tube* utilizes this phenomenon to allow a trace to remain on a screen after the signal which has caused it is discontinued.

photoresist   The process, utilized in etching *semiconductor* devices, of selectively removing the oxidized surface of a silicon *wafer* by masking the part which is to be retained.

pickup   Interference from an extraneous circuit.

pico-   Prefix meaning 10^{-12}, as in picosecond, one million-millionth of a second.

pixel   Synonymous with *pel*.

PL/1   A *high-level language* developed to combine features required for commercial languages and scientific languages.

PLA   Abbreviation for *programmed logic array*.

place   A *digit position* within a set of digits corresponding to a given power of the *radix*.

plant   To place the result of an *operation* in a *location* for later use.

playback head   Synonymous with *read head*.

PL/M   A *high-level language* developed for microprocessor systems programming.

plotter   A visual display or board on which a graph is represented automatically as a function of one or more variables.

PMOS   Abbreviation for P-channel metal oxide *semiconductor*, in which the electrical current is a flow of positive charges. Contrasted with *NMOS*.

pn boundary   A transition region between *p-type* and *n-type* materials where the donor and acceptor concentrations are equal.
Also known as pn junction.

pn junction   Synonymous with *pn boundary*.

p-n-p transistor   A *transistor* consisting of two *p-type* crystals separated by an *n-type* crystal.

pointer   A *word* which contains the *address* of another *location* which has a logical relationship.

polarized plug   A plug so designed that it can be inserted only when it is in one predetermined position.

polarizing slot   A slot in the edge of a *printed circuit board*, designed to accept a specific type of connector.
Also known as indexing slot.

Polish notation   A method of representing statements in *Boolean algebra* in which the *variables* precede the *operators*; it combines conciseness and avoidance of ambiguity.

poll   A systematic method of testing each *channel* on a multipoint circuit in order to accept incoming data or locate a free channel, thus avoiding *contention*[2] when several *terminals* share channels.

polling characters   A set of *characters* peculiar to a specific *terminal*; response to these characters in a *poll* indicates whether or not the terminal requires servicing.

polling interval   The time period between *polling* operations, assuming that no data is transmitted from the *terminal* being polled.

polyphase sort   A *merge sort* in which sorted *subsets* are distributed among a proportion of available *storage* devices in accordance with a Fibonacci series. The subsets are then merged on the remaining storage devices, and the process is repeated until one sorted set remains.

pop   Synonymous with *pull*.

port   A place of entry to or exit from a *central processor*, dedicated to a single data *channel*.

portability   A *program* is portable if it can be used on more than one system. In theory, programs written in *high-level languages* are portable, but the natural desire of computer manufacturers to manifest the superiority of their equipment usually means that only *subsets* of languages are truly portable.

positional notation A form of *number system* in which a set of digits represents a number in such a way that both the position of each digit as well as its value are significant.

position pulse Synonymous with *commutator pulse*.

positive logic A positive voltage level is defined as 'one', while a negative voltage level is defined as 'zero'.

post To *update* a *record*.

post-mortem routine A *diagnostic routine* used to provide information about the functioning of a *program*.

p-pulse Synonymous with *commutator pulse*.

precision A measure of the degree of exactness; high precision implies a high degree of exactness but with no implication as to *accuracy*.

prefix notation A notation for representing *logical operations* in which expressions are written without brackets and the extent of the *operators*[3] is indicated by their relative positions. Contrasted with *infix notation*.

Prestel The name given by British Telecom to the first public *viewdata* system.

presumptive address Synonymous with *base address*.

presumptive instruction Synonymous with *basic instruction*.

PRF Abbreviation for pulse repetition frequency. ◊ *pulse repetition rate*.

printed circuit A circuit in which the interconnections are made by conductive strips printed or etched on an insulating board.

printed circuit board An insulating board on to which a circuit has been printed or etched.
Also known as card, chassis, PC board, plate.

printer An *output device* capable of converting signals into printed form.

print format A representation of the way in which data is to be printed, showing column widths, position of page numbers, headings, etc.

printout The printed pages output by a *printer*.

priority indicator In *data transmission*, code signals which define the relative importance of a *message*, resulting in the formation of a queue, each item of which is handled in order of importance.

private line A *channel* or circuit furnished to a user for his exclusive use.

Also known as leased line.

problem definition The presentation of a problem for computer solution in a formal, structured way.

problem orientated language A *program language* designed for convenient handling of programs related to a particular type of problem, e.g. commercial, scientific, engineering design.

process chart Synonymous with *systems flowchart*.

process control The use of a computer to control directly a physical process, e.g. the automatic regulation of a level of pollution in a factory environment, the automatic control of the operations in a chemical plant.

processor Synonymous with *central processor*.

processor limited A system condition which occurs when the time taken to complete a process is dictated by the time taken by the *central processor* rather than the time taken by *peripheral units*. Contrasted with *peripheral limited*.

product The result of multiplying two *factors*.

production run An operational *run* of a fully tested, proven system.

productive time Time spent in fault-free, uninterrupted *production runs*.

program 1. A set of *instructions* prepared to provide a computer solution to a problem, by directing a computer to carry out a desired sequence of operations. 2. To prepare such a set of instructions.

program address counter Synonymous with *instruction register*.

program cards *Punched cards* containing *program instructions*, usually with one instruction in each card.

program compatibility The result of *portability*, where a *program* can be *run* on two different computers.

program compilation The process of using a *compiler*.

program control The function of organizing the operations of a device *on-line* to a *central processor*.

program controller The *central processor* unit which organizes the *execution* of *instructions*.
Also known as program control unit.

program control unit Synonymous with *program controller*.

program counter Synonymous with *control register*.

program flowchart Synonymous with *flowchart*, and used to emphasize a contrast with *systems flowchart*.

program generator Synonymous with *generator*.

program library A set of tested *routines*, some developed by the user and some by the computer manufacturer, and all likely to be used in the installation concerned.

programmable read-only memory (PROM) An integrated circuit of *read-only memory* which can be programmed by a user (i.e. after manufacture) by means of a *hardware* device known as a PROM programmer (◊ *programmer unit*). A programmable read-only memory is usually designed so that a proportion of the available words is used to provide a read-only data *storage* capacity and a proportion can be written into (or *blown*) by the executing program.

program maintenance The process of keeping *programs* up to date by correcting errors, making changes as requirements change and altering the programs to take advantage of new *peripheral units*.

programme ◊ *program*.

programmed check A *check* carried out by the use of *program instructions*.

programmed dump A *memory dump* made as a result of an *instruction* providing a snapshot of memory for use in a later *debugging* process.

programmed halt A *halt* in a *program* which takes place when the program meets a *halt instruction*.
Also known as coded stop.

programmed logic array (PLA) That area of a *chip* whose function is to implement the decoding of *instructions* and the logic control steps.

programmer 1. A person capable of producing a working *program*. Sometimes distinguished from a *coder* by the implication that a programmer is capable of designing a program while a coder is limited to writing instructions to meet a design. 2. Synonymous with *programmer unit*.

programmer-defined macro A *macroinstruction* used frequently in a *program* and therefore defined by a *programmer*[1] at the beginning of a specific program.

programmer unit A *hardware* device which provides the means for *programming programmable read-only memory (PROM)*, utilizing a control program which allows *instructions* to be *blown* and verified. PROM contents can be copied into a *random-access memory* bank and edited.
Also known as PROM programmer.

programming The process of producing, from a *program specifi-*

cation, a set of *instructions* which have been tested and shown to make a computer carry out the activity defined in the specification.

program modification   The process of performing arithmetic and logic *operations* on *instructions* and *addresses* during a *program* in such a way that their actions are altered.

program origin   Synonymous with *initial address*.

program register   Synonymous with *instruction register*.

program-sensitive fault   A *fault* which results from a particular combination of *instructions*.

program specification   A detailed definition of the processes and procedures to be carried out by a *program*; this definition acts as the basis of work for a *programmer*[1].

program step   A single operation in a *program*; usually an *instruction*.

program storage   That area of *main memory* in which a *program* may be placed; protection devices are often used to prevent accidental alteration of the contents of such an area. Sometimes a designated *chip* is reserved for the storage of programmed *instructions*.

program test   The *running* of a sample problem with a known answer, thus allowing an opportunity to discover errors in a *program*.

program testing   The process of *running* a *program* with *test data* in order to check that it is correctly performing expected operations.

PROM   Acronym for *programmable read-only memory*.

PROM blaster   Synonymous with PROM blower (◊ *blow* and *programmer unit*).

PROM blower   ◊ *blow* and *programmer unit*.

PROM burner   Synonymous with PROM blower (◊ *blow* and *programmer unit*).

PROM programmer   ◊ *programmer unit*.

prompt   A message provided by an *operating system* calling for *operator*[1] action.

proof list   A *printout* showing *instructions* and *narrative* as originally prepared and the *object code* produced from them.

propagated error   An *error* which takes place in one *operation* as a result of a *propagating error* in another operation.

propagating error   An *error* which takes place in one *operation* and results in errors in other operations.

propagation loss The energy lost by a signal during the process of passing between two points on a circuit.

propagation time The time taken by an electrical signal to travel through or along a medium between two points on a circuit.

protected location A *location* reserved so that the contents cannot be altered without a special procedure; data can be read from such a location but not written to it, and unplanned modification of the contents is therefore prevented.

PRR Abbreviation for *pulse repetition rate*.

protocol A set of conventions governing the format of messages to be exchanged between one process and another communicating with it. For example, *central processors* which need to communicate may operate at different speeds, on different *word* lengths, with different *access* controls, etc., and protocols need to be established so that each can recognize and act on signals being transmitted between them.

proving Testing a machine in order to demonstrate that it is free from *faults*, usually after corrective maintenance.

pseudo-code A code or language which must be translated into *machine code* before it can be *executed* on a computer; usually a mnemonic code. Distinguished from *pseudo instruction*.

pseudo instruction A group of characters arranged in the same general symbolic form as an *instruction*, but not capable of being performed as an instruction in the running of a *program*.
Also known as quasi instruction.

pseudo-random sequence A sequence of numbers generated as a result of a defined process and therefore not truly random, but which is considered to be satisfactorily random for a given calculation.

p-type The characteristic of a *semiconductor* in which the hole density exceeds the density of electrons. During crystal growth pure *silicon* is *doped* with impurity atoms such as boron to make p-type silicon, with positive charges due to the absence of an electron; they readily accept an electron from an adjacent atom, thus causing the hole to appear to move. Contrasted with *n-type*.

pull To remove an element from a *stack*. Contrasted with *push*.
Also known as pop.

pulse An abrupt and relatively short change in voltage, either positive or negative, resulting in the conveyance of data in a circuit.
Also known as impulse.

pulse code   A code in which digits are represented by means of sets of *pulses*.

pulse code modulation   (PCM) The process of sampling a modulating signal periodically, quantizing (◊ *quantization*) the sample and transmitting it as a digital *binary* code.

pulse repetition frequency   (PRF) The rate at which pulses are repeated in a *pulse train* which is independent of the time interval over which it is measured.

pulse repetition rate   (PRR) The average number of *pulses* per unit of time.

pulse stretcher   A circuit capable of extending the duration of a pulse.

pulse train   A sequence of *pulses*.

punch   1. To make a hole in a specific position of a *punched card* or piece of *paper tape*. 2. A device which will make these holes.

punch card   Synonymous with *punched card*.

punched card   A piece of cardboard cut to a standard size in which data can be punched in the form of holes in accordance with a specified code. The position of the holes can be sensed by machines which can then transfer the data in the form of pulses to a *central processor*.

Also known as punch card.

purge date   A date written to a data medium on or after which the file may be released and the data may be *overwritten* by new data.

push   To add an element to a *stack*. Contrasted with *pull*.

Also known as put.

pushdown list   A list in which the last item entered becomes the first item of the list, and each of the other items is 'pushed down' one position in the list.

pushdown stack   A *register* which stores *operands* and controls register transfers on a last-in first-out basis.

pushdown store   A *store* which operates to maintain a *pushdown list*.

Also known as cellar.

pushup list   A list in which each new item is entered at the end of the list without altering the relative positions of earlier items on the list.

put   Synonymous with *push*.

Q

quad Four separately insulated conductors twisted together to form a structural unit used in a cable.

quantization The process of dividing the range of values of a wave into a finite number of subdivisions, each of which is known as a *quantum*.

quantum A subdivision made as a result of *quantization*.

quantum clock The means of timing an interval of processing time in a *time sharing environment*[3].

quartz crystal A thin slice cut from quartz and ground to a thickness at which it will vibrate at a required frequency when supplied with energy.

quartz delay line An *acoustic delay line* in which fused quartz is used as the medium for delaying sound transmission.

quasi instruction Synonymous with *pseudo instruction*.

queue A set of transactions awaiting processing; a list which allows the insertion of data at one end and removal of data (or deletion) at the other.

Also known as wait list.

queue discipline The choice of method adopted for servicing transactions in a *queue*, e.g. first-in first-out or last-in first-out.

quick-disconnect A type of connector which allows rapid locking and unlocking of the two connector halves.

quiesce To reject new jobs in a *multiprogramming* system, while continuing to process jobs already entered.

quintet A *byte* consisting of five *binary* elements; a five-*bit* byte.

quoted string A *character string* enclosed by quotation marks, perhaps to represent a value including *blanks*[1].

quotient The result obtained from dividing two numbers, the *dividend* being divided by the *divisor*.

R

rack A *chassis* or frame on which a *microprocessor* can be mounted.

radix The base of a number system, indicating the positional representation (◇ *positional notation*) of the system. For example, in the *binary* system the radix is two, in an *octal* system it is eight, in a decimal system it is ten, and in a *hexadecimal* system it is sixteen.

Also known as base[1].

radix notation The representation of numbers to a specific *radix*. Also known as base notation.

radix point The location of the index which separates the integral part and the fractional part of a number, marked in the decimal system by the decimal point (a dot in English usage, a comma elsewhere), in the *binary* system by a binary point.

RAM Acronym for *random-access memory*.

RAM refresh Dynamic *random-access memory* units require a periodic *refresh* operation to ensure that data is retained, since *bits* are represented by a capacitive charge.

random access A method of providing or achieving *access* in which the time to retrieve data is constant and independent of the *location* of the item addressed previously. ◇ *random-access memory*.

Also known as direct access.

random-access memory (RAM) *Memory* which provides *access* to any *location*, allowing data to be *written* to or *read* from any location. The retrieval speed is independent of the address. Dynamic RAM units require stored data to be *refreshed*; static RAM units do not need refreshing but require continuous power.

range The difference between the highest and lowest values of a function or quantity.

rapid-access loop A section of *storage* which has a faster *access time* than the remainder of the storage medium.

raster The coordinate grid of a *terminal screen*, dividing the display area into discrete positions.

raster count The number of coordinate positions which may be addressed on a *terminal screen*; the horizontal count is the number across the width of a screen, and the vertical count is the number across the height.

raw data *Data* which has not been processed.

reactive mode Method of communication between a *terminal* and a *central processor* in which each entry causes an action but does not necessarily generate an immediate (interactive) response to the terminal.

read To interrogate the contents of *memory* without changing the contents; to transfer data from one form of *storage* to another.

reader Any device able to *read* data.

read head An electromagnet used to *read* data from a magnetic medium.

Also known as reading head or playback head.

reading head Synonymous with *read head*.

read-only memory A *memory* circuit in which the stored pattern is *blown* during manufacture and cannot be changed by the user or altered by *program*; used to provide a means of storing a fixed program in a *microprocessor*. ⬦ *programmable read-only memory*.

readout Display of processed information on a *terminal screen*. Contrasted with *printout*.

read rate Number of units of data (e.g. *words*, *blocks*, *fields*) capable of being *read* by an *input device* in a given period.

read time The interval between the start of transcription from a *storage* device and the completion of transcription.

read/write channel A *channel* between a *peripheral unit* and a *central processor*.

read/write head An electromagnet used to *read* from or *write* to a magnetic medium.

Also known as combined head or combined read/write head.

real time The period of time taken in processing a solution to a problem when the time is not greater than the time taken by a physical process to which the problem relates; for example, the computations involved in guiding an aircraft to a runway, with adjustments being made as the aircraft lands. Data necessary to the execution of a transaction is affected by the result of the process itself.

reasonableness check Tests made on data to establish that it falls within a prescribed range.

receiver A device able to accept incoming electrically transmitted signals.

receiver isolation The *attenuation* between two *receivers*.

recompile To *compile* a *program* again, usually after *debugging* or because the program needs to be *run* on a different type of computer.

reconfigure To change the components of a computer system and the interconnection of the components.

reconstitute To restore a *file* to the condition which pertained at an earlier stage of processing, perhaps as a result of a *restart* procedure after a *dump*.

record A *data processing* unit representing a *transaction*[3] or a part of a transaction, made up of a group of related *fields*.

record blocking The grouping of *records* into *blocks* which can be read and/or written to *magnetic tape* in one operation, thus increasing the efficiency with which the tape is used.

record count The number of *records* in a file, used as control information.

record format The contents and layout of a *record*.

record head Synonymous with *write head*.

recoverable error An error which does not prevent acceptable *execution* of a *program*.

recovery The restoration of a system after *failure*; recovery procedures are designed to isolate *errors*.

rectifier A device capable of converting an alternating current into a direct current.

recursion The continuous repetition of an operation or set of operations.

recursive subroutine A *subroutine* able to *call*[1] itself.

red-tape operation An *operation* which does not in itself contribute to a result, but which is necessary to enable data to be processed. Red-tape operations tend to be specific to an application, while *housekeeping* operations are more general.

reduction The process of transforming *raw data* into condensed, organized processable data.

reduction cascading Moving from one level to another with an increasing level of detail. Contrasted with *expansion cascading* which moves from detail to broader and broader classification.

redundancy The employment of more units than is necessary, thus providing an element of safety in the event of failure. For example, extra *bits* attached to a data item are used in a redundancy check; a second *central processor* is known as redundant although its function may be to provide instant back-up if the first should fail.

151

Also known as resilience, but with the implication that redundancy provides resilience.

redundancy check A *check* which requires the presence of extra *characters* or *bits* to allow the automatic detection of errors. The extra characters do not themselves contribute to the information and are therefore described as redundant, although they do, of course, perform a valuable function.

redundant character ◊ *check character*.

reel 1. A roll of *paper tape*. 2. The spool or spindle used for holding a *magnetic tape*. 3. Magnetic tape and spool, collectively described as a reel.

re-entry The continued entering of a *program* or *routine* before the *execution* of that program or routine is completed, provided that neither the external *parameters* nor any *instructions* are modified during execution.

reference address Synonymous with *base address*.

reference list A *printout* produced by a *compiler* to identify *instructions* as they appear at the end of a *run*, indicating their *locations*.

reformat To change the representation of data from one format to another.

refresh To supply data over and over again to meet the requirements of a dynamic *read-only memory* or a *raster* scan display.

Also known as regenerate.

regenerate Synonymous with *refresh*.

regenerative memory Any *storage* device which needs to be *refreshed* if the contents are to be saved from gradual disappearance.

Also known as Cheshire Cat store.

register A specific *location* in *memory* used for one or more *words* for use during arithmetic, logic or transfer operations, e.g. *index register*, *instruction register*. Data is usually held in a register only long enough for a specific purpose, and registers usually have a capacity equal to the word length of the *central processor* concerned.

rejection Synonymous with *Nor operation*.

relative address A number, contained in the *address* part of an instruction, which must be added to a *base address* to provide an *absolute address*.

Also known as floating address.

relative coding Writing *instructions* using *relative addresses*, thus avoiding the need to consider the *absolute addresses* required when writing a program in several *segments*.

relocatable routine   A *routine* with *instructions* written in relative code (⊳ *relative coding*) so that they can be located and acted on in any part of *memory*.

relocate   To move a *routine* from one area in *memory* to another, modifying the addresses so that the routine can still be executed from the new area.

remainder   That part of the result obtained from a *division* which remains when the *dividend* has been divided by the *divisor* to give the *quotient*.

remote   Away from a *central processing* point.

remote batch processing   The sending of data and *programs* in *batches* to a *central processor* by means of communication devices.

remote data concentration   The *multiplexing* of a number of low-activity or low-speed lines or terminals on to one high-speed line between a *remote terminal* and a *central processor*.

remote job entry   (RJE) The entering into a *remote terminal* of data and *programs* for transmission to a *central processor* for processing. Results may be transmitted back to the originating terminal.

remote terminal   A *terminal* at a different location from the *central processor* it is accessing.

repertoire   The set of *operations* which can be represented in an operation code; the set of *instructions* which a given computer is capable of executing.

replication   A form of *redundancy* in which each *hardware* unit is supported by an identical unit for use in the event of failure of the original unit.

report generation   The output of information drawn from a *file* or files as a result of specification of content and layout of the required *printout* and the format of the files concerned; the specification *parameters* are presented to a *report generator*, thus obviating the need to prepare a special print program.

report generator   A general-purpose *program* designed to print out information from *files* on presentation to it of *parameters* specifying the format of the files concerned plus the format and content of the printed report, and any rules for creating totals, page numbering, etc.

Also known as report program generator, RPG.

report program generator   (RPG) Synonymous with *report generator*.

rerun To repeat the execution of a *program*, usually after the detection of an *error* condition.

rescue dump The recording of the complete contents of *memory* on a *backing store*, so that the *data*, intermediate results and the status of *instructions* can be reconstituted in the event of power or machine failure.

reserve To allocate a *memory* area and/or *peripheral units* to a particular *program* operating in a *multiprogramming* system.

reserved word A *label* or *word* which may not be used by a *programmer*[1] because it has a special significance to the *compiler*, which would recognize the word and take some other action than that expected by the programmer.

reset To return a *register* or *location* to zero or to a specified initial condition.

reset pulse A *drive*[2] pulse used to control the state of a *storage* cell (⬦ *binary cell*), specifically one that restores a cell to zero.

resident Existing permanently in *memory*, for example a resident *compiler* or *executive program*. Non-resident routines must be called into memory from a *backing store*.

residue check A check carried out to test the validity of an arithmetic operation; each *operand* is accompanied by a *remainder* obtained by dividing this number by n.

resilience 1. The capacity of a system to continue to run in spite of the fact that a component has failed; running in *crippled mode*. 2. Synonymous with *redundancy*, but with the implication that redundancy provides resilience.

resist In the manufacture of *printed circuit boards*, the material used to protect appropriate parts of the conductive material from the etching action.
Also known as resist-etchant.

resist-etchant Synonymous with *resist*.

resistor A device which restricts the flow of current into a circuit.

resistor-transistor logic (RTL) Logic carried out by the use of *resistors*, with *transistors* producing an inverted output.
Also known as transistor-resistor logic (TRL).

resonance The sympathetic vibration of a circuit to a signal.

resource A unit in a *configuration*[2] which can be separately allocated.

response time The time elapsed between the initiation of an operation (e.g. an inquiry at a *terminal*) and a result (e.g. receipt from a central computer of a response at the same terminal). The time includes all processing between initiation and result, and in the example given would include transmission time to the central computer, processing time at the central computer (including *access* time to appropriate *files*) and transmission time back to the terminal.

restart To re-establish the process of *executing* a *routine* after a *program* or data error or machine malfunction. Restarting usually involves returning to a *checkpoint* placed at appropriate intervals so that, in the event of failure, a job can be resumed without the need to start again at the beginning of the *run*.

restore 1. To set a *counter, register, switch* or *indicator* to its initial condition. 2. To regenerate a charge periodically in a volatile *storage* medium; synonymous with *refresh*.

result The outcome of an *arithmetic* or *logical operation* performed by an *operator* on one or more *operands*.

retentivity The property of a material to retain magnetic flux.

retrieval The process of searching for, selecting and extracting data contained in a *file* or files.

retrieve To carry out *retrieval*.
Also known as fetch.

retrofit To change an existing *routine* or system to accommodate a new section or an alteration to an existing section, and to make corresponding changes in related routines or systems.

return address Synonymous with *link*.

return instruction An *instruction* which has the function of returning control to a main *routine* after the execution of a *subroutine*.

reverse bias A voltage applied to a p-n crystal in such a way that the positive terminal is applied to the n section of the crystal and the negative terminal to the p section.

reverse recovery time The time required for the current or voltage to reach a specific state after being switched from a *forward current* condition to a *reverse bias* condition.

reversible magnetic process A process of flux change within a magnetic material whereby the flux returns to its previous condition when the magnetic field is removed.
Also known as reversible process.

reversible process Synonymous with *reversible magnetic process*.

rewind To return to the beginning of a *magnetic tape* or *paper tape*.

rewrite To regenerate data in those *storage devices* where the process of *reading* data results in its destruction.

RF Abbreviation for radio frequency.

RFI   Abbreviation for radio frequency interference.

RF modulator   A device which modulates the frequency of a received carrier signal.

right justify   To *store* a data item in such a way that it occupies consecutive positions beginning at the extreme right-hand end of the particular *location*. Similarly, to print items, or display them on a *terminal screen*, in such a way that the right-hand margin is straight.

right shift   To displace digits in a *word* to the right, having the effect of *division* in *arithmetic shift*.

ring   A *chained list* in which the *pointer* of the last item points to the first item.

ring shift   Synonymous with *logical shift*.

ripple-through carry   Synonymous with *high-speed carry*.

rise time   The time required for the leading edge of a pulse to rise from 10 per cent to 90 per cent of its final value.

RJE   Abbreviation for *remote job entry*.

RO   Abbreviation for receive only – equipment that can receive but not transmit data.

robot   Any device equipped with sensors capable of detecting input signals and environmental conditions and with reacting and guidance mechanisms; capable of performing calculations on the input data in accordance with a stored program, and consequently able to run itself.

robotics   An area of *artificial intelligence* usually applied to the industrial use of *robots* in repetitive tasks.

roll-back   The process of returning to a *checkpoint* during a *restart* procedure.

roll-in   The process of returning to *main memory* data that had previously been transferred to *backing store*.

roll-out   To transfer all or part of the contents of *memory* to *backing store*.

roll-out/roll-in   A technique for temporarily increasing the availability of *main memory* by moving data or *programs* to *backing store*, using the area thus vacated and then returning the data or programs to their original *locations*.

rollover   A keyboard encoding mechanism allowing a specified number of keys to be depressed at the same time without error.

ROM   Acronym for *read-only memory*.

rounding error   An error in a *result* caused by *rounding off*.

round off To adjust the value of digits at the least significant end of a number to reduce the effect of *truncation*.

round robin A cyclical *multiplexing* procedure, allocating *resources* in fixed-time slices.

routine A set of *instructions* arranged in a planned sequence in order to direct a computer to carry out a set of operations; generally considered to be part of a *program*, but also used as a synonym for program.

routing Sending messages in a communications system, directing the messages along switched paths.

row A line of horizontal elements in a matrix.

row binary A method of representing *binary numbers* in a *punched card* by regarding consecutive positions in each *row* as consecutive digits in a binary number.

RPG Abbreviation for report program generator. ◊ *report generator*.

RTL Abbreviation for *resistor-transistor logic*.

rubout Synonymous with *erase*.

run The execution of a *routine*, *program* or *suite* of programs, usually complete in some aspect (e.g. the solution of a particular problem) and thus particularly related to a *batch processing* operation.

runaway The condition which arises when an input to a physical system is subject to a sudden, undesirable increase or decrease.

run book Documentation necessary for assembling the necessary inputs for operating a job, including operating instructions and *flowcharts*.

run time The time during which an *object program* is *executed*.

S

sample To obtain and record the value of a *variable* at periodic or random intervals.

satellite computer A computer connected remotely or locally to a central computer and carrying out defined processing tasks, either independently of the central computer to serve local needs, or subordinately to the central computer to carry out such tasks as *compiling*, *editing* and controlling *input* and *output* functions. In the last case, the satellite is acting as a *front-end processor*.

saturation The condition of magnetism of a material beyond which no further magnetization is possible.

saturation noise *Errors* introduced into data as a result of *saturation*.

SBC Abbreviation for single board computer.

scan To examine each part in sequence; this may be each item in a *list*, each *record* in a *file*, each point of a display, each *input* or *output* channel of a communication link.

scanner A device which *samples* or interrogates the status of a process or *file*, initiating action appropriate to the data obtained in the scanning process.

scanning rate The rate at which a *scanner samples*.

scatter load A method of assigning *locations* in *memory* in such a way that data in non-sequential segments of memory is perceived as being loaded sequentially.

scatter read The process of locating data in non-contiguous memory areas as it is being *read* into the system.

schema A description of the structure of a *data base*[1].

scissor To remove elements of a graphic display.

scope Abbreviation for oscilloscope.

scratch pad A *memory* area used as a temporary working area for intermediate results.

screen 1. That part of the surface of a *cathode ray tube* which is visible to the user of a *terminal*. 2. To make an initial broad selection before undertaking a detailed selection process.

screen read The process of allowing a message displayed on a *terminal screen* to be retransmitted to a microprocessor or *peripheral device*, so that data can be formatted for *storage*[1] or for *editing*.

scroll   To move the contents of a *screen* up or down, a line at a time.

SDLC   Abbreviation for synchronous data link control.

search   1. The process of identifying a given *record* before retrieval. 2. To carry out such a process.

Also known as seek.

searching storage   Synonymous with *associative storage*.

secondary store   Synonymous with *backing store*.

second generation   Applied to computers using transistors. Contrasted with first generation (using thermionic valves) and third generation (integrated circuits).

second source   An alternative supplier of an item of *hardware* or *software*. The availability of a second source is often an important purchasing consideration.

section   Synonymous with *segment*.

sector   A defined area of a *track* or *band*[1] on a magnetic recording medium such as *magnetic disk* or *magnetic drum*.

security   The state achieved by *hardware*, *software* or *data* as a result of successful efforts to prevent damage, theft or corruption. In a *data base management system* the term is also often taken to embrace privacy and thus relates to the protection of data against accidental corruption during updating, against unusual and possibly fraudulent updating and against unauthorized access to data protected by specific levels of confidentiality.

seek   Synonymous with *search*. But ⟡ *cylinder*.

seek area   Synonymous with *cylinder*.

segment   A division of a *routine*, capable of being *stored* and *run*, together with appropriate *instructions* for *branching* to another segment. The division is usually of a size capable of being treated as an *overlay*, read into *store* and *executed* at one time (although sometimes a segment has within it *subsegments* which overlay each other). Also known as chapter, section.

select   To follow a path as a result of testing a condition.

selective dump   A *dump* of the contents of a specified area of *memory*.

selective fading   Signal fluctuation, in which the components of the signal fade unequally.

selector   A switching device which allows a condition to be tested and a path to be followed as a result of the test.

self-adapting   Pertaining to the capability of a device or *program* to change the characteristics of its performance in response to changes in its environment.

self-checking code   Synonymous with *error-detecting code*.

self-resetting loop   Synonymous with *self-restoring loop*.

self-restoring loop   A *loop* which includes *instructions* to cause all *locations addressed* during the loop to be restored to the condition that obtained when the loop was entered.

Also known as self-resetting loop.

semantic   Pertaining to the relationships between symbols and what they represent.

semantic error   The use of an incorrect or ambiguous symbol, or the omission of a symbol, in the preparation of a *program*.

semicompiled   Converted by a *compiler* from a *source language* into *object code*, but not yet including *subroutines* required by the source language program.

semiconductor   A material with an electrical conductivity which is between that of a metal and an insulator. The electrical conductivity is sensitive to the presence of impurities and increases or decreases as the temperature around it increases or decreases. These properties mean that the material is suitable for rectifiers, detectors and gates in computer circuits. ⊂⊃ *hole*, *n-type*, *p-type*.

sensitivity analysis   The determination of the interdependence or response of output values by a test of a range of input values.

sentinel   Synonymous with *flag*.

separator   A *character* which *delimits* logical units of data.

septet   A seven-*bit byte*.

sequence   1. To place a group of items into a defined order, in accordance with identifiable *keys*. 2. A set of items arranged in such an order.

sequence check   A test to ensure that an ordered set is in the expected *sequence*.

sequence control register   A *register* which acts as a counter and determines the order in which *instructions* are *executed*.

Also known as sequence counter, sequence register.

sequence counter   Synonymous with *sequence control register*.

sequencer   A module in a *bit-slice microprocessor* which holds the next *microprogram address*.

sequence register   Synonymous with *sequence control register*.

sequential access   A method of *access* in which data is accessed in the *sequence* in which it is *stored*, after all preceding items have been accessed. *Magnetic tape* requires sequential access.

serial Pertaining to data or *instructions* stored or transmitted sequentially, in *sequence*.

series The connection of circuit elements end to end in a string.

service bit A *bit* used in data transmission in connection with the process rather than the data itself.

service program Synonymous with *utility program*.

servomechanism A *feedback* system in which the output influences the input.

set 1. To place a *storage* device into a specified state, usually not zero or blank; e.g. to give a *bit* the value of one. 2. A collection of items; usually a collection with something in common.

set-up time 1. The time required to change a signal from one state to another. 2. The time required to prepare equipment for operation.

sexadecimal Pertaining to sixteen; as in sexadecimal notation, a notation using the base sixteen. More usually, hexadecimal.

sextet A *byte* of six *bits*.

SHF Abbreviation for super high frequency (between 3000 and 30,000 megaHertz).

shield A conducting housing placed around a magnetic field.

shift 1. The operation of moving the elements of an ordered set of units (*bits*, *characters*, *digits*) one or more places to the left or right. ◊ *arithmetic shift*. 2. To move elements in such a way.

shift pulse A drive pulse which initiates a *shift*.

shift register A *register* whose contents can be moved to the left or right as a result of a *shift*.

short out To make inactive by the interposition of a low resistance path around a device.

sideband A frequency band on either side of a carrier frequency when a set of frequencies modulates the carrier frequency.

sign An indicator which distinguishes positive from negative quantities.

signal A conveyor of *data* – the physical embodiment of data.

signal distance The number of *bit* positions which differ in two *binary words* of the same length; for example the following two binary words differ in two digit positions, and the signal distance between them is therefore 2:

100111
110101

Also known as Hamming distance.

signal regeneration The process of restoring a *signal* to an original specification.

Also known as signal reshaping.

signal shaping The process in a *modem* which confines a *signal* to a specific frequency band.

signal standardization The generation of a *signal* from another; the generated signal meets specified conditions of amplitude, shape and timing.

sign bit A *sign digit* composed of a single *bit*.

sign check indicator An *indicator* set, according to specification, on a change of *sign* or when a sign is positive or when a sign is negative.

sign digit A *digit* whose value designates the *sign* of a number.

signed field A *field* containing a number which incorporates a *sign digit*.

sign magnitude A method of *binary* representation where the most significant *bit* is used for the *sign* and the rest of the number represents the absolute value.

sign position The position in a number which holds the *sign digit*.

silicon An element which is a semiconductor and, when mixed with iron or steel to provide magnetic properties, is used for transistors in metal oxide *semiconductor* technology.

silicon-gate Pertaining to metal oxide *semiconductor* technology using *silicon* as the semiconductor for the *gate* of the transistor.

Silicon Gulch An area in California which has attracted many *semiconductor* manufacturing plants.

Also known as Silicon Valley.

silicon on sapphire (SOS) Technology in which sapphire is used as a *substrate*; sapphire is a true insulator, not a semiconductor, and its use results in a reduction of parasitic capacitance.

Silicon Valley Synonymous with *Silicon Gulch*.

simple buffering The association of a *buffer* with a single *input* or *output file* throughout a process, thus providing the ability to obtain the simultaneous performance of input/output operations and *central processor* activities.

simplex Capable of transmission in one direction only. ⟡ *duplex* and *half-duplex*.

simulate 1. To represent physical problems by mathematical formulae. 2. In *programming*, to use a *routine* on one computer in such a way that that computer operates as nearly as possible like a different computer.

simulator A *program* which *executes object* programs generated on a machine other than the one for which the program was designed. This allows *debugging* before, for example, a program is committed to *read-only memory*.

simultaneity The ability to allow *central processor* activities to take place at the same time as *input/output* activities.

single-address code Synonymous with *single-address instruction*.

single-address instruction An *instruction format* which contains one operand *address* only.

Also known as single-address code.

single-length working The representation of *binary* numbers so that the value of each number can be contained in a single *word*.

single-pass program A *program* which results in the production of the problem solution or completed process after one *run*.

single-shot circuit *Circuits* or *logic elements* which carry out *signal standardization*.

Also known as one-shot circuit.

sink current The current drive capability of a specific logic group.

SIP Abbreviation for single in-line package. Contrasted with *dual in-line package*.

sizing The process of evaluating what resources and facilities are needed to achieve a particular level of service or to provide a solution to a specific problem.

skeletal code A set of *instructions* some parts of which must be completed each time the code is used.

skip To pass over one or more *instructions*, *jumping* to another instruction in the sequence.

slab A crystal from which *slices*[1] are cut.

slave A unit which is under the control of another unit.

slave tube A *cathode ray tube* connected to another in such a way that both tubes perform identically.

sleeping sickness The failure of a *transistor* as a result of moisture collecting on the base.

slew rate *Signal* response rate.

slice 1. A wafer of *silicon*. 2. Synonymous with *bit-slice*. But ➪ *time slice*.

slow death Gradual deterioration of the characteristics of a *transistor* or other device.

SLSI Abbreviation for super large scale integration: more than 100,000 *transistors* on one *chip*.

smart terminal A *terminal* which is capable of a certain amount of processing without using the power of the computer to which it is connected. The processing power of the terminal is available to the user at the terminal end, and he may *program* the terminal to meet his own needs. There is an implication that a smart terminal has rather less local processing capability than an *intelligent terminal*.

smoke test The process of switching on a device for the first time. If all is well there is no smoke and the implication is that a sight check will indicate if the machine is in working order.

snapshot debug A *debugging* technique in which a *programmer* specifies the start and end points of *segments* for which he requires a *snapshot dump*.

snapshot dump A *dump* of selected parts of *memory*, allowing the contents of *registers* and memory locations to be examined as part of a *debugging* process.

SNOBOL A *high-level language* orientated to the processing of character *strings*.

socket One end of a circuit, capable of receiving a plug to complete the circuit.

Also known as jack.

soft error An unpredictable fault, usually concerned with *software*. Contrasted with *hard error*.

soft-fail Synonymous with *fail soft*.

soft keyboard A display arranged on a *terminal screen* in the form of a keyboard; a *light pen* directed at the appropriate key will cause the *character* represented by that key to be *input*.

software 1. All *programs* written to be executed on *hardware*, including *operating systems*, utility programs and *application* programs. 2. In a more specialist sense, those programs written by a computer manufacturer to provide basic facilities for users: all programs except those written by the user to meet his specific requirements.

software-compatible Pertaining to a computer which can accept and *run programs* written for another specific computer.

sonic delay line Synonymous with *acoustic delay line*.

sort To order data items according to the identifying rules or an identifying *field* or *key* in each item.

SOS Abbreviation for *silicon on sapphire*.

source 1. A device which emits signal power. 2. Abbreviation for *source code*.

source code A *program* in a language written by a *programmer*[1]; the source code cannot be directly *executed*, but must first be *compiled* into *object code*.

source deck Synonymous with *source pack*.

source document   An original document from which data is prepared in a *machine-readable* form.

source language   A *programming language* for preparing *source code*.

Also known as synthetic language.

source machine   A machine capable of carrying out the *compilation* of *source code*; contrasted with *object computer* on which the *object code* will be *run*.

source pack   A *pack* of *punched cards* containing *instructions* in *source code*.

Also known as source deck.

source program   A *program* written in *source code*.

space   An empty unit of data storage, represented by binary 0.

space character   Synonymous with *blank character*.

space suppression   The process of preventing a normal movement of paper in a *printer* after a line of characters has been printed.

span   The difference between the highest and lowest values in a *range* of values.

sparse array   An array in which zero is the predominant character.

special character   A character which is neither a letter nor a numeral, e.g. !, ", /.

Also known as additional character, symbol.

specific address   Synonymous with *absolute address*.

specification   A statement of requirements.

specific code   Synonymous with *absolute code*.

specific coding   ⟡ *absolute code*.

spooling   The process of releasing *memory* by temporarily storing data on *backing store* until it is required for a further processing operation.

squoze pack   Synonymous with *condensed pack*.

stack   An area of *memory* reserved for the storage of data, *subroutines* and *interrupt* managements; a stack is designed on last-in first-out principles and is manipulated by *instructions* to *push* or to *pop*. But ⟡ *pushdown stack*.

stack pointer   A *register* which holds the *address* of the top of a *stack*.

stand-alone   A device or system capable of operating in its own environment with no dependence on any other device or system.

standard interface   Agreed interconnection standards of circuits and *input/output channels* which allow any *peripheral unit* meeting the standards to connect to any *central processor* meeting the standards.

stand by   A set of duplicate equipment for use if the original set fails.

star program   Synonymous with *blue ribbon program*.

start bit   A *bit* whose presence indicates the start of asynchronous (⟡ *asynchronous working*) *serial* transmission of data. Contrasted with *stop bit*.

start time   Synonymous with *acceleration time*.

statement   Any expression which can be input to a *compiler*, including a *source language instruction*, a *narrative* statement and a *directive* controlling the operation of the compilation.

statement number   A serial number given to each *statement* in a *program* written in a *source language*.

static dump   A *dump* carried out when a *program* reaches the end of a *run*, or at another major milestone during a run.

static memory   *Memory* which is non-volatile and does not require to be *refreshed*, so long as power is applied.

status register   A *register* which contains information about the condition of a functional unit or peripheral device, e.g. *interrupt* state or a 'paper-low' condition on a *printer*.

step   Synonymous with *instruction*.

stochastic   Containing an element of chance.

stop bit   A *bit* whose presence indicates the end of asynchronous (⟡ *asynchronous working*) *serial* transmission of data. But ⟡ *halt instruction*.

stop code   Synonymous with *halt instruction*.

stop instruction   Synonymous with *halt instruction*. But ⟡ *stop bit*.

stop time   Synonymous with *deceleration time*.

storage   1. The process of storing (⟡ *store*). 2. Any device or medium capable of accepting data and retaining it, so that it can be retrieved and used when required. Storage can be considered as *memory*, *backing store* and *source documents*, with intermediate storage devices linking these three.

storage allocation   The allocation of *locations* in *memory* to specific types of *data*. Storage allocation is carried out during preparation of a *program*, and is performed by a *compiler*.

storage capacity   The amount of information which can be held in a *storage device*, usually expressed as a number of units of data (*words*, *characters*).

storage density   The number of units of data which can be stored in a unit length or area of a *storage* medium.

storage device   A device used as a *backing store* (✧ *storage*); examples are *magnetic tape*, *magnetic disk*, etc.

store   To place data into a *storage device*.

stored program   A *program* which is wholly contained in *memory*, which is capable of being altered in memory and which is stored along with the data on which it is to operate.

straight-line coding   *Programming* which avoids the use of *loops* by repeating a set of *instructions* instead of *branching* repeatedly to the same set, thus increasing the speed of *execution* of the program.

string   1. A set of items which has been arranged into a *sequence* according to a rule. 2. Any set of consecutive *characters* present in *memory*.

string break   In *sorting*, the condition which occurs when there are no more *records* with *keys* higher than the highest key so far written.

string length   In *sorting*, the number of *records* in a *string*[1].

string manipulation   The process of manipulating groups of contiguous *characters* in *memory*, treating them as units of data.

subroutine   A well-defined part of a *program* which carries out a logical part of the functions of the complete program and which can be called into action whenever the particular part is required. A subroutine requires as a main *parameter* an *address* to which it returns control after it has carried out its task.

subroutine library   A collection of *subroutines* which can be called by and used in different *programs* when required.

subscript   A notation written below and usually after an individual member of a set of items, in order to distinguish it from the others of the same name. A subscript character shows the *location* of elements in an *array*.

subsegment   A part of a *segment*.

subset   A group of items which itself belongs to a larger group.

substrate   The physical material on which a circuit is fabricated.

subtracter   A device carrying out the function of *subtraction* using digital signals. The device receives three inputs representing *minuend*, *subtrahend* and a *carry* digit, and provides two outputs representing the *difference* and a carry.
Also known as full subtracter.

subtraction   An *arithmetic* operation in which one *operand* – the

167

subtrahend – is subtracted from another– the *minuend* – to form the *difference*.

subtrahend In *subtraction*, the subtrahend is subtracted from the *minuend* to give the *difference*.

suite A number of *programs* related to each other and *run* consecutively to enable a processing job to be completed.

sum A result obtained by the *addition* of an *addend* and an *augend*.

support chip A component in a system needed for complete operation, but additional to the main *central processor*.

suppression The elimination of certain components of an emission, e.g. the prevention of the printing of selected *characters* when specified conditions occur. ◊ *zero suppression*.

surface barrier The potential barrier across the surface of a *semiconductor* junction.

swap 1. To keep a job on *backing store* and periodically transfer it to *main memory* for *execution* during a specifically allocated period of time. 2. The process of making such a transfer.

switch 1. To open, close or direct the path of electric current. 2. A device for opening, closing or directing the path of electric current. 3. To alter the state of a *bit*. 4. To use a *branch instruction* (which selects one of a number of paths) as a result of the setting of an *indicator*.

switched-message network A communications system in which data can be passed between any users of the network.

switch insertion The process of inserting *data* or *instructions* by means of manually operated *switches*[2].

symbol A *character* accepted by convention or specification as representing a concept such as a quantity, relationship, operation or process.
Also known as special character.

symbolic address An *address* in a *source language*, becoming an *absolute address* when the *program* has been *compiled*.

symbolic code Synonymous with *symbolic instruction*.

symbolic instruction An *instruction* in a *source language*.
Also known as symbolic code.

symbolic language Any computer language used by a *programmer*[1] preparing *source code*.

symbolic programming Writing a *program* in a *source language*.

symbol table A *table* constructed by an *assembler* or *compiler* to relate *symbolic addresses* to their *absolute addresses*.

symmetric difference Synonymous with *Exclusive-Or* operation.

sync Abbreviation for *synchronization*, as in *sync character*.

sync character A *character* transmitted to establish satisfactory character synchronization in synchronous communication.

synchronization The process of bringing into step two waves, signals or functions.

synchronizer A unit which acts as a *buffer*, and maintains synchronization by counteracting the effects of transmitting data between units which operate at different rates.

synchronous Pertaining to operations performed under the control of equally spaced signals from a *clock*.

synchronous system A system in which all activities are synchronized by means of a common *clock pulse*.

synchronous working Performing a sequence of operations under the control of equally spaced signals from a *clock*. Contrasted with *asynchronous working*.

syntax The grammatical rules which govern the structure of a language; in particular, the rules for forming *statements* in a *source language*.

synthetic address Synonymous with *generated address*.

synthetic language Synonymous with *source language*.

sysgen The process of *generating* an *operating system* in a user's *environment*. Short for system generation.

system chart Synonymous with *systems flowchart*.

system generation Synonymous with *sysgen*.

systems analysis The investigation and recording of existing systems and the design of new systems.

systems analyst A person trained to undertake the tasks of *systems analysis*.

systems definition A complete description, fully documented, of a problem and its solution or proposed solution.

systems flowchart A *flowchart* in which the *flowchart symbols* represent specific clerical and computer procedures. Contrasted with *program flowchart*.
Also known as flow-process diagram, system chart.

systems software *Intimate software*, including *operating systems*, *compilers* and utility software (⟡ *utility program*). Contrasted with *applications software*.

T

tab   1. Synonymous with *label*. 2. Abbreviation for *tabular language*.

table   A set of data arranged in *memory* as an *array* in such a way that the data may be retrieved by search according to an *algorithm* (table look-at) or by searching for a specified *key* (table look-up).

table look-at   ◊ *table*.

table look-up   ◊ *table*.

tabular language   A method of stating programming requirements as *decision tables*.

Also known as tab.

tag   One or more *characters* associated with a *record* in order to provide identification or to contain information about an overflow record.

tail   A *flag* denoting the end of a *list*.

takedown   The process of completing one operating cycle (e.g. removing *magnetic tapes* and *printout* from *peripheral units*) before preparing the equipment for *loading* the next job.

takedown time   The time required to complete a *takedown* operation.

tape   ◊ *magnetic tape* or *paper tape*.

tape deck   A device for controlling the handling of *magnetic tape*; consists of a transport mechanism which drives the tape past a *read head* and a *write head*, and allows automatic rewinding.

Also known as deck, magnetic tape deck, magnetic tape unit, tape drive, tape transport.

tape drive   Synonymous with *tape deck*.

tape label   A *record* at the beginning and end of a reel of *magnetic tape* which provides details about the *file* stored on the tape. ◊ *header label* and *trailer label*.

tape loadpoint   The position on a piece of *magnetic tape* at which reading or writing can begin.

tape mark   A *character* on a *magnetic tape file* which divides the file into a new section.

Also known as control mark.

tape punch   A device for punching holes in *paper tape*.

tape reader   A device capable of reading *data* recorded as holes punched in *paper tape*.

tape transport Synonymous with *tape deck*.

target computer The computer on which *object code* is to be run. The object code may be compiled on a computer of a *configuration* which differs from that of the target computer.

target language Synonymous with *object language*.

target program Synonymous with *object program*.

task A *program* or part of a program capable of being presented as a single unit of work in a *multiprogramming* or *multiprocessing* environment.

TDM Abbreviation for *time-division multiplexing*.

telecommunication The transmission and reception of data in verbal, coded or pictorial form over radio circuits or transmission lines by the use of electromagnetic signals.

teleprinter A device which can transmit or receive data to or from a distant point by means of a telegraphic circuit.

teleprocessing Processing by a combination of computers and telecommunications facilities – the connection of remote facilities to a central computer; the term is registered by IBM.

teletext Television screen message services either broadcast like *Ceefax* and *Oracle* or transmitted by cable.

Telex An international network of *teleprinters*.

Telpak A wide-band *channel* service which allows communication by combined voice and data channels.

tens complement A *radix complement* of a decimal number.

tera- A prefix denoting one million million.

terminal A *peripheral* device with a visual display and, usually, a keyboard, thus allowing data to be output (as screen display) and input (through the keyboard). Terminals are *dumb*, *smart* or *intelligent*, depending on the degree of local processing capability. Also known as inquiry display terminal, VDI, VDT, VDU, video.

terminal area The part of the conductive pattern of a circuit to which electrical connections can be made.

terminal node The final *node* of a *tree*, with no following nodes.

ternary Pertaining to three; a ternary number representation system uses the digits 0, 1 and 2 and the *radix* is three.

test alphabetic A *validity check* designed to ensure that input is appropriately alphabetic.

test bed A *software package* used for *program* testing.

test data Data prepared to test the performance of a *program* in usual and unusual conditions; expected results are also prepared so that

171

these may be compared with the actual results produced by the program.

test for blanks A *validity check* designed to ensure that appropriate *fields* are blank.

test numeric A *validity check* designed to ensure that input is appropriately numeric.

test program A *program* designed to use and check the different *hardware* units of a computer.

testrad A group of four pulses or *bits*, used to express a decimal or hexadecimal (base sixteen) number in *binary* form.

testrode A four-electrode electronic device.

test run A *run* carried out to check that a *program* is operating correctly; during the run *test data* generates results for comparison with previously prepared results.

text The information part of a *message*, excluding *characters* or *bits* needed for the actual transmission of the message.

text editing The process of locating and modifying data already in a *file*, thus allowing data presented in a raw state to be prepared for printing out in, for example, an appropriate *justified*[1] column width.

thick film Pertaining to hybrid integrated circuits made of layers of magnetic material deposited on a ceramic *substrate*.

thin film Pertaining to a *storage* medium consisting of a very thin layer (a few millionths of an inch thick) of magnetic material deposited in a vacuum on a plate of non-magnetizable material such as glass.

thread A group of *beads* which have been strung together for testing.

threaded file Synonymous with *chained file*.

threaded tree A *tree* which contains extra *pointers* to other *nodes*.

three-address instruction An *instruction* in which three addresses are specified as part of the *instruction format*.

three-input adder An *adder* with three inputs, *addend*, *augend* and *carry*.

threshold A value specified to control the output from a *threshold element*.

threshold element A *logical element* with one output signal and several input signals, each of which carries a specified weight. The output signal is dependent on the input signal being greater or less than a given value, known as the *threshold*.
Also known as decision element.

throughput The speed of productivity of a machine, system or procedure, measured as units of information appropriate to the process under consideration.

time-delay circuit A circuit capable of delaying the transmission of an impulse for a specific period.

time-division multiple access A technique of merging signal streams in traffic of data to and from satellites.

time-division multiplexing (TDM) A *multiplexing* technique of allocating a communications channel for a specific short period to a number of different devices. Each user appears to be receiving uninterrupted service.

time quantum The amount of time given to each user in a *time sharing* system.

time-scale factor The relationship between the time taken for a physical event and the time taken for the simluation of that event by an *analog computer*. The ratio is usually stated as simulation: actual.

time sharing A method of allowing one device to be used for two or more concurrent operations, e.g. several *terminal* devices using the input, processing and output facilities of a *central processor* apparently simultaneously. In fact, the central processor operates momentarily to carry out a finite series of steps for one device, then another, until the operations are completed.

time slice A prescribed interval during which a job can use a specified device without being interrupted.

toggle 1. Synonymous with *flip-flop*. 2. An operating switch, e.g. for data entry to a *central processor*.

trace A *diagnostic routine* used to carry out a check on another *program* and locate errors. The output may be selected *instructions* from the program being checked and may also include results obtained when such instructions were *executed*.

track A channel on a magnetic medium; that part which passes a *read/write head*.

traffic intensity A measurement of the difference between insertion and deletion rates in a *queue*.

trailer label A *record* identifying the end of a *file* stored on a *magnetic* medium.

trailer record A *record* at the end of a group of records, providing control data relating to the group.

transaction 1. An event which results in a record being generated or updated in a *data processing* system. 2. The record so generated. 3. A set of exchanges between a *terminal* and a *central processor*.

transaction file Synonymous with *change file*.

transaction record Synonymous with *change record*.

transaction tape A magnetic tape containing *transactions*[2] or *change records*.

Also known as change tape.

transceiver A *terminal* device capable of both transmitting and receiving signals from a telecommunications circuit.

transcribe To copy data from one medium to another; either including a translation process or not.

transducer A device capable of converting energy from one form to another, and made to flow from one or more transmission system to another transmission system.

transfer control The action taken by a *branch instruction* when it transfers control from one part of a *program* to another part.

transfer function A mathematical expression relating the output of a *closed loop servomechanism* to the input.

transfer instruction An *instruction* which copies data from one part of *memory* to another or transfers control from one part of a *program* to another.

transient Used as a noun, an unstable state reverting intermittently to stability.

transistor A *semiconductor* used as a switch or as an amplifier; has three electrodes (emitter, base and collector), which are attached to a *wafer* of semiconducting material treated so that its properties are different at the point of each electrode.

translate To change data from expression in one form to expression in another without a significant change of value or meaning.

translater ⬦ *translator*.

translation The process of converting data from expression in one form to expression in another without a significant change in value or meaning.

translator A *program* capable of *translating statements* written in one *programming language* to the *format* of another.

transponder A radio or satellite *transceiver* which responds to a specific interrogation signal by transmitting identifiable signals.

trap An automatic *branch* operation activated when *illegal instructions* are executed or illegal *locations* are *addressed*.

tree A data structure which allows selection by *reduction cascading* or (when all members of a group are to be selected) by *expansion cascading*. The graphic representation, made by connection of the *nodes* – which have no cycles – resembles a tree.

tree sort A sort which exchanges data items treated as *nodes* of a *tree*.

triad A group of three *characters* or *bits*.

trigger level The minimum receiver input capable of causing the transmitter of a *transponder* to emit a signal.

trim-pot A *resistor* which can be adjusted manually.

triple-length working Performing arithmetic operations on numbers which require three *words* in order to provide the necessary precision.

TRL Abbreviation for transistor-resistor logic. ◊ *resistor-transistor logic*.

trouble shoot To search for, locate and correct errors in a *program* or machine malfunction.

truncation Cutting off the least-significant digits of a number, thus sacrificing precision to achieve greater speed or simplification.

trunk 1. A single message circuit between two switching centres. 2. Synonymous with *bus*.

truth table A mathematical table which shows the Boolean (◊ *Boolean algebra*) relationship of *variables*, demonstrating the results obtainable from various combinations of values. Truth tables show possible combinations of input and the consequent output labelled as 0 and 1.

truth value The *input* and *output* quantities in a *truth table*.

TTL Abbreviation for transistor-transistor logic; bipolar circuit logic taking its name from the way the basic components are connected.

tube Synonymous with *screen*.

two-address instruction An *instruction* in which the *addresses* of two *operands* are specified as part of the *instruction format*.

two-input adder A *logical element* which accepts two digital input signals (a digit of a number and an *addend* or a *carry*) and provides two output signals (a *carry* digit and a digit for the *sum*).

two-input subtracter A *logical element* which accepts two input signals (a digit of a number and a borrow digit or one representing the *subtrahend*) and produces two digital outputs, a borrow digit and a digit for the *difference*.

two-level subroutine A *subroutine* containing another subroutine.

two-plus-one address An *instruction format* in which two *addresses* are used to specify separate *operands*, while a third address is used for the location of the result.

twos complement A *radix complement* for *binary notation*.

TVT Abbreviation for television typewriter; a low-cost means of displaying data on a television set.

two-valued variable Synonymous with *binary variable*.

U

UART Abbreviation for universal asynchronous receiver transmitter; allows the conversion of serial to parallel and parallel to serial transmission.

UHF Abbreviation for ultra high frequency; the range extending from 300 to 3000 megaHertz.

ultraviolet erasing Erasable programmable read-only memory (*EPROM*) *chips* may be erased by exposure to high-intensity shortwave ultraviolet light.

unconditional branch An *instruction* which transfers control to another part of the *program*, irrespective of the results of previous instructions. Contrasted with *conditional branch instruction*. Also known as unconditional jump, unconditional transfer.

unconditional jump Synonymous with *unconditional branch*.

unconditional transfer Synonymous with *unconditional branch*.

underflow A result whose value is too small for the range of the number representation being used. Contrasted with *overflow*.

union Synonymous with *Or operation*.

unipolar A signal in which the same electrical voltage polarity is used to represent different logical states. Contrasted with *bipolar*.

unmodified instruction Synonymous with *basic instruction*.

unpack To recover original data from a form in which it has been packed, separating combined items into separate *words*. Contrasted with *pack*.

unwind To show explicitly and in full all the *instructions* used during a *loop*.

update To process a *file* by applying *transactions* to it in order to amend, add or delete *records* in accordance with specified procedure.

upwards compatible ◊ *compatible*.

USASCII Abbreviation for United States of America standard code for information interchange.

user program A *program* written specifically for or by a particular user; contrasted with *utility program*.

USRT Abbreviation for universal synchronous receiver-transmitter.

utility program   *Programs*, usually provided by *hardware* manufacturers or *software* houses, to carry out standard operations on *files*;
such operations are not related to the specific contents of the files,
but are concerned with such routine general activities as transferring data from one medium to another, listing of *storage* contents,
copying files, etc. Contrasted with *user program*.

Also known as service program.

UV   Abbreviation for ultraviolet. ⟡ *ultraviolet erasing*.

V

validate To apply *validity checks* in order to reduce the number of errors entering a data processing system.

validity check A check based on prescribed limits within which data must fall and which is designed to identify invalid or unreasonable items.

variable Any *symbol* or *character* which may assume different values during a *run*.

VDI Abbreviation for video display input or visual display input. ⟡ *terminal*.

VDT Abbreviation for video display terminal or visual display terminal. ⟡ *terminal*.

VDU Abbreviation for visual display unit. ⟡ *terminal*.

vector A quantity which has magnitude and direction; a structure which allows location by means of a single subscript or index.

vectored interrupt An *interrupt* which carries either a *branch address* or a *peripheral unit* identifier.

vector transfer A means of communication linkage between two *programs*; a *table* is fixed in relation to that program for which it is the transfer vector.

Veitch diagram A chart showing *truth table* data, used in the design of circuits simulating Boolean operations (⟡ *Boolean algebra*).

Venn diagram A chart in which circles or ellipses are used to indicate logic relationships between categories.

verifier A machine used to *verify* automatically.

verify To check a method of recording data either by representing the action or by using another method and comparing the results.

vertical redundancy check (VRC) A check on parity (⟡ *parity bit*) to establish an odd number of *bits* in an even parity system or an even number of bits in an odd parity system.

very large scale integration (VLSI) Over 10,000 *transistors* on each *chip*.

VHF Abbreviation for very high frequency – between 30 and 300 megaHertz.

video 1. Synonymous with *terminal*. 2. The brightness and colour data fed to a terminal.

video bandwidth   The maximum number of dots per second that a television screen can display.

videotex   Synonymous with *viewdata*.

viewdata   Interactive *data base*[1] search system utilizing telephones, computers and television sets to make large computer data bases available to public access, usually by *display menu* selection. Also known as videotex.

virgin medium   A medium with no *data* whatsoever, not even *housekeeping* data. Contrasted with *empty medium*.

virtual   Pertaining to a conceptual, rather than physical, presence.

virtual address   An *address* generated by a *programmer* to reference what he regards as his address area, without regard to the physical *memory locations*. Computers with *virtual memory operating systems* are able to translate a virtual address into an *absolute address*.

virtual memory   A *memory* management facility under certain *operating systems* which allows a *programmer*[1] to make use of the storage resources without having to consider the physical constraints of *memory* or the possible requirements of other applications.

visual display unit   Synonymous with *terminal*; sometimes reserved for terminals with no input facilities.

VLSI   Abbreviation for *very large scale integration*.

voice channel   A circuit of adequate *bandwidth* to allow transmission of speech quality signals; a bandwidth of 0–3000 cycles per second.

volatile memory   *Memory* which cannot retain data when the power is switched off.

VRC   Abbreviation for *vertical redundancy check*.

W

wafer A thin slice from a *silicon* ingot; the slice is the basis of the silicon *chip*.

wait list Synonymous with *queue*.

wait state The internal state of a processing unit when a synchronizing signal has not yet been received.

wait time Pertaining to a *storage* unit, the interval during which a processing unit is waiting for data to be transferred to or from a store.

Also known as latency.

wand A stick-like device used to recognize optically coded labels.

warm-up time The interval between the energizing of a device and the beginning of the application of its output characteristics.

waste instruction Synonymous with *do-nothing instruction*.

wire wrap board A *circuit board* using the technology for connections whereby wire is wrapped many times round a square pin to make contact.

word A group of *characters* representing a unit of data and occupying one *storage location*; each word is processed as an entity and is treated by a *control unit* as an *instruction* and by an *arithmetic unit* as a quantity.

word processor A *text editing* device designed for the preparation, storage and dissemination of text initiated on typewriter-like units.

word time The length of time required to move one *word* from one *storage* device to another.

work area An area of *memory* used for the temporary storage of data during processing.

Also known as working storage (WS), workspace.

workspace Synonymous with *work area*.

wraparound On a *terminal screen* the continuation of an operation from the last character position in display to the first position in display; data which cannot be displayed at the bottom of a screen because the screen is full is displayed at the top, overwriting existing data.

write To record data, copying it from one form of storage to another.

write head An electromagnet used to *write* data to a magnetic medium.

Also known as record head.

write rate The maximum speed at which the spot on a *screen* can produce a satisfactory image.

write time The interval between the start of transcription to a *storage* device and the completion of transcription.

writing head ◊ *write head*.

WS Abbreviation for working storage. Synonymous with *work area*.

X

x punch   A hole in the x position of a *punched card*, usually the second row from the top although in some notations the top row is known as x.

x-y plotter   Synonymous with *data plotter*.

Y

yield The usable *chips* in a production batch.

yoke A group of *read/write heads* fastened together and consequently capable of being moved together.

y punch A hole punched in the *y* position of a *punched card*, usually the top row, although in some notations the second row is known as *y*.

Z

zap To *erase*, as in *PROM*-zapping. Contrasted with *blow*.

zero condition The state of a magnetic cell when it represents zero. Also known as zero state and nought state.

zero elimination Synonymous with *zero suppression*.

zero fill To replace blank characters in an area of *memory* with the representation of *zero*, without changing the meaning of the data.

zero-level address Synonymous with *immediate address*.

zero state Synonymous with *zero condition*.

zero suppression The elimination before printing of non-significant zeros, e.g. those to the left of significant digits.
Also known as zero elimination.

More About Penguins
And Pelicans

For further information about books available from Penguins please write to Dept EP, Penguin Books Ltd, Harmondsworth, Middlesex UB7 0DA.

In the U.S.A.: For a complete list of books available from Penguins in the United States write to Dept CS, Penguin Books, 625 Madison Avenue, New York, New York 10022.

In Canada: For a complete list of books available from Penguins in Canada write to Penguin Books Canada Ltd, 2801 John Street, Markham, Ontario L3R 1B4.

In Australia: For a complete list of books available from Penguins in Australia write to the Marketing Department, Penguin Books Australia Ltd, PO Box 257, Ringwood, Victoria 3134.

The Penguin Reference Series

The Penguin Atlas of African History
Colin McEvedy

The Penguin Atlas of Ancient History
Colin McEvedy

The Penguin Atlas of Medieval History
Colin McEvedy

The Penguin Atlas of Modern History (to 1815)
Colin McEvedy

The Penguin Atlas of World History (Volumes 1 and 2)
Hermann Kinder and Werner Hilgemann

Atlas of World Population History
Colin McEvedy

The Penguin Book of Mathematical and Statistical Tables
R. D. Nelson

The Penguin Companion to Literature:
1 British and Commonwealth Literature
Ed. David Daiches
2 European Literature
Ed. Anthony Thorlby
3 United States and Latin America Literature
Ed. Mottram et al
4 Classical and Byzantine,
 Oriental and African Literature
Ed. R. Dudley and D. M. Lang

The Concise Cambridge Italian Dictionary
Barbara Reynolds

Penguin Reference Series

A Critical Dictionary of Psychoanalysis
Charles Rycroft

The Penguin Dictionary of Archaeology
Warwick Bray and David Trump

The Penguin Dictionary of Architecture
(Completely Revised Edition)
John Fleming, Hugh Honour, Nikolaus Pevsner

A Dictionary of Art and Artists (Fourth Edition)
Peter and Linda Murray

The Penguin Dictionary of Biology (Seventh Edition)
M. Abercrombie, C. J. Hickman, M. L. Johnson

The Penguin Dictionary of Building (Revised Edition)
John S. Scott

The Penguin Dictionary of Civil Engineering
(Third Edition)
John S. Scott

The Penguin Dictionary of Commerce
Michael Greener

The Penguin Dictionary of Computers (Second Edition)
Anthony Chandor

The Penguin Dictionary of Decorative Arts
John Fleming and Hugh Honour

A Dictionary of Economics
Graham Bannock, R. E. Baxter, Ray Rees

The Penguin Dictionary of English and European History
E. N. Williams

A Dictionary of Fairies
Katherine Briggs

A Dictionary of Geography (Fifth Edition)
W. G. Moore

Penguin Reference Series

The Penguin Dictionary of Geology
D. G. A. Whitten with J. R. V. Brooks

The Penguin Dictionary of Historical Slang
Eric Partridge, Abridged by Jacqueline Simpson

A Dictionary of Modern History 1789–1945
A. W. Palmer

The Penguin Dictionary of Modern Quotations
(Second Edition)
J. M. and M. J. Cohen

The Penguin Dictionary of Physics
Ed. Valerie H. Pitt

A Dictionary of Psychology
James Drever

The Penguin Dictionary of Quotations
J. M. and M. J. Cohen

The Penguin Dictionary of Saints
Donald Attwater

The Penguin Dictionary of Science (Fifth Edition)
E. B. Uvarov, D. R. Chapman, Alan Isaacs

The Penguin Dictionary of Surnames (Second Edition)
Basil Cottle

A Dictionary of the Theatre
John Russell Taylor

The Penguin Dictionary of Twentieth Century History
Alan Palmer

Encyclopedia of Mountaineering
Walt Unsworth

The Penguin Encyclopedia of Places
W. G. Moore

The Penguin English Dictionary (Third Edition)
G. N. Garmonsway

Facts in Focus (Fifth Edition)
Compiled by the Central Statistical Office

Penguin Reference Series

A Handbook of Management (Third Edition)
Thomas Kempner

The International Thesaurus of Quotations
Rhoda Thomas Tripp

The Penguin Medical Encyclopedia (Second Edition)
Peter Wingate

Medicines: A Guide for Everybody (Third Edition)
Peter Parish

Mind the Stop
G. V. Carey

The New Penguin Dictionary of Electronics
E. C. Young

The New Penguin Dictionary of Music (Fourth Edition)
Arthur Jacobs

The New Penguin World Atlas
Ed. Peter Hall

Roget's Thesaurus
(Entirely rewritten within Roget's original structure)

The Penguin Russian Course
Compiled by J. L. I. Fennell

The Penguin Shorter Atlas of The Bible
Luc. H. Grollenberg

Usage and Abusage
Eric Partridge

Who's Who in the Ancient World
Betty Radice